Travel-Trailer Homesteading Under $5,000

Revised and Expanded Second Edition

by Brian Kelling

Breakout Productions
Port Townsend, Washington

This book is sold for informational purposes only. Neither the author nor the publisher will be held accountable for the use or misuse of the information contained in this book.

Travel-Trailer Homesteading Under $5,000
Revised and Expanded Second Edition
© 1999 by Brian Kelling

Published by:
Breakout Productions, Inc.
PO Box 1643
Port Townsend, WA 98368

Photos by Brian Kelling

ISBN 1-893626-05-9
Library of Congress Card Catalog 99-63627

Contents

Preface

The object of this book is to demonstrate how to purchase and set up a complete RV homestead for under $5,000, land and trailer included.

You'll have all the comforts of home: power, heat, pressurized water, refrigeration, and a septic system.

Sound too good to be true? It's not. I did it, and I'll show you how.

I started with a 21-foot travel trailer on 5 acres in southern Colorado. Everything was paid for, and I had all I needed in creature comforts.

Since this book was first published in 1995, I purchased and set up a mobile home, adapting all the same ideas and techniques as from the travel trailer. This second edition contains a chapter devoted specifically to this.

Either way you go, there are only four prerequisites to get started: the money, a pickup truck, tools, and the willingness to live a new life. But before you sell everything and start off, I'd suggest you read this entire book.

Letters

I'm glad to be able to report that of the mail I've received about the first edition, all was positive, and most was a hearty "Thank you!" One gal said I'd "put into words what she'd been dreaming about doing for years."

A few were along the lines of, "Do you know how I could buy property in Vancouver? (Arizona, Idaho, etc.)" My answer is usually the same: You should go there first, look around, and buy what you feel comfortable with.

A couple people had gotten travel trailers and were packing up to leave. They just wrote to say how happy they were, and I'm glad for them.

One woman wrote to say she wanted to *meet* me....

And, as I suspected would happen, several people wrote to tell me that they are already living as I do, which of course was no great surprise to me. One of them is now a very good friend of mine.

But by and large, I'm sad to say, the majority of letters have come from wannabes, people who only dream about getting out of the rat race. I feel for them, having been in the same boat myself at one time.

It's good for people to dream, but a close friend once told me, *"Dreams without planning and action are nothing short of fantasy."*

He was so right. So stop dreaming — just do it!

At any rate, thank you all, good luck, and *mucho gusto!*

Cost Breakdown

The following figures are based on my situation:

```
Land.......................................................... $2,195
Trailer........................................................... 1,200
Skirting............................................................. 75
Generator ........................................................ 200
Heat................................................................ 105
    (Woodstove, 80)
    (Flue/accessories, 25)
Propane tank.................................................... 241
Solar power ..................................................... 692
    (Panels 215)
    (Batteries 260)
    (Platform 70)
    (Inverter 80)
    (Regulator 67)
Septic System..................................................... 70
Cistern.............................................................. 49
    (Pump 19)
    (Barrels 15)
    (Pipe 15)
Air pump ............................................................ 5
TV antenna......................................................... 23
Mailbox.............................................................. 7
```

```
TOTAL ....................................................... $4,862
```

Tools You'll Need

Tools are an important part of setting up the homestead, and you can do practically nothing without them. You should gather as many as you can; sooner or later, you will use them all. Visit garage sales for most of this, but I recommend buying a new chain saw.

The following is a basic, must-have list:
- Chain saw
- Circular saw
- Jigsaw
- Handsaws
- Hacksaw
- Drill and bits
- Phillips bits for drill
- Screwdrivers
- Tape measure
- Level
- Power cords
- Caulking gun
- Wood rasp
- Tin snips
- Shovels
- Axes
- The usual assortment of automotive tools

And any other basic carpentry, plumbing, or electrical tools you can lay your hands on. I mean it!

Chapter One
How This Came to Be

Six years ago, I sat in my construction-office trailer, pulling my hair out and popping Tagamet. It was an insanely hectic $70-million project. When the phone, fax, pager, or radios weren't going off — and no one came by for answers — I'd just sit there and stare at the photograph on my wall. I could have done it for hours: wishing, hoping, dreaming... but these brief respites were never more than moments long.

Oh yeah, the money was good, you know it. And there were times when I really enjoyed making the machine run. I owned a nice home in the suburbs (me and the bank, that is), drove new vehicles, bought what I felt like, and paid a lot of bills. But there was no time.

Evenings — when I went home late for dinner — were good because they gave me a chance to catch up on the never-ending supply of paperwork such a job produces and demands. I had an office there, too, where in my spare time I detailed a hardware schedule for 900 doors on this very word processor. I wanted to be writing books instead, but somehow that just never got done — there being no time.

"Free time" was a thing of the past, or so it seemed. And I resented not having enough time to pursue my dreams.

Travel-Trailer Homesteading Under $5,000

Through quick glances on weekdays and Saturday mornings, there was the picture, always there, never changing. Sometimes, I even thought about it in church. It was a thousand miles away, yet it was always with me, occupying a special place in my free moments of thinking. I can imagine my father saying, "Can you believe that? Didn't even have time to *think!*"

But when I *did* have time to think, I'd dream about that place in the picture. It really was "gentle on my mind," to quote Glen Campbell.

But it was just a picture, you say.

Yes, it was just a picture. A picture of horses grazing on open country. There were no houses visible, nor fences, stoplights, or shopping malls; no "expressways," police stations, hospitals, or convenience stores. Just the horses, the open country, and behind them, the fourth-tallest mountain in the state of Colorado.

Four basic colors made the picture. In the foreground, the brown of the mid-winter valley floor, dotted with the horses. Beyond that, where the land goes up, the thick green of exactly a million trees. Above the timberline, the pure white of deep, cold snow. The bluest of big Western skies capped it off.

To me, it was a picture of incredible grandeur. And right there, where those horses grazed, that was my property, although I never got to think about it much. There were always meetings to attend, contracts to write, quotes to review, and people to pressure. In short, there was work to be done, but somehow I swore I'd get out of this rat race.

When it finally got to be too much, I asked for my vacation. "Vacation! You can't take a vacation, there's too much going on!" they said. I told them the truth, I was so wound up I couldn't even take a dump, and I was going whether they liked it or not. Cripe, the electrician's manager had a heart attack, at

53! They raised hell with me, and I again told them the truth — I'd quit if I didn't get it, and I meant it.

After a day's rest I was on a plane to Denver, where I rented a car and drove the four-and-a-half hours to my property. There was something I had to do.

By evening I stood on my land and watched the setting sun light a *hundred miles* of mountains. It was so magnificent, so quiet! I almost cried. Not a sound....

For nearly a week I stayed at a motel, reading the paper and checking out the town. I'd talk with people and find out the costs of things. Every day I'd return to my land and walk the property lines, thinking. There was a question that needed answering, and I wouldn't leave until I got it. Squatting down, I'd crumble the dirt between my fingers, as if I'd find the answer there.

But it *wasn't* there, and it wasn't in the town. It was in me. And the question was, could I really do it? Could I really leave a solid career, sell my home, and just take off for the country? Could I start all over again? Inside, it felt irresponsible somehow, and I was sure people would say that. After all, I was finally getting somewhere, making more money than ever before. My pension was vested, and grew by the day. How could I throw away what I'd worked so hard to get? *Just a few more years,* I'd tell myself, and I'd be set.

Just a few more years....

Then one day, I saw the horses again. They trotted up to see who the newcomer was. While they sniffed and milled around, I patted the paint's neck like an old friend.

When they left, I just stood and watched them go, wandering at will for miles, no halters on, and freer than I'd ever been. No bars held them in; there was no place they had to be. It was surely a sight... and I had my answer.

Back in the pressure cooker, everything was easier now. I kept it to myself, but my days were numbered. The end of the job was near, and managers were scrambling for a new place to go. When they asked where I was going next, I'd simply point to the picture — "right there."

They were *incredulous*. "What do you mean?"

"What are you going to do out there?"

"As little as possible."

"Brian," they'd tell me, "you're throwing your career out the window!"

Nonplussed, I'd smile and reply, "That's *exactly* what I'm doing."

I have never regretted my decision.

Chapter Two
The Land

Figure 1
The land

Choosing your land is probably your most important consideration, and there are many things to take into account.

For starters, where would you *like* to live? To me, this is the most important question.

 5

Then, where can you *afford* to live? Where can you find a piece of suitable land for $2,500?

Is the county zoned? Are mobile homes allowed?

What are the taxes? How far is it to town?

Does the county maintain the road? (Assuming there is a road.)

Is it accessible in the winter? Do you have a four-wheel-drive vehicle?

What's the climate like? Is there a lot of sun?

How far to water? How far to firewood?

Is the ground suitable for a septic system?

What will you do after the homestead is in? Will you work?

I would start with the question, "Where do you want to live?" Start regionally; say, the West or the South. From there, narrow it down to a particular state. Then investigate different areas.

In my instance, I knew exactly where I wanted to live, in the San Luis Valley of southern Colorado. I had already purchased a 5-acre tract in Alamosa County a few years back for a total of $2,195. I paid $295 down and made monthly payments of $50 until the loan was paid off. I preferred to have the land, and everything else for that matter, paid in full, but making payments is an option. It would drop your initial amount substantially from the $5,000 we are talking about in this book. But you have to be able to make the payments.

My taxes are $52 a year, and there is a building inspector to deal with, but I found him most reasonable. For instance, mobile homes are allowed in Alamosa County, but travel trailers are not. However, my trailer is one of many. There are even a few buses. One guy I know built his entire house — complete with artesian well — without a single permit. There's even a straw-bale house down the road a few miles.

Building inspectors are powerful people in big cities, but that's not always the case in small towns. I did eventually buy a building permit for a rock house, and this got him off my back. Also, by that time, I had my septic system installed, and that pacified him further.

Anyhow, I love the West, and particularly this part of Colorado. It's sunny almost every day, the views are fantastic, people are friendly, and land is cheap.

The San Luis Valley is the largest mountain valley in the world, roughly the size of Massachusetts. The Rocky Mountains run all the way around this valley, and the elevation here at the floor is quite high (7,550 feet).

There are still some places available for $2,500, especially in Costilla County, Colorado, where land is cheaper. It's a favorite for homesteading, as are most of the farther out places. Several years ago, I bought a 5-acre piece there for $1,200, and sold it for $1,500. Recently, a realtor I met in town sold a 5-acre lot in Alamosa County for $500, and it's in the artesian zone. Some area agents deal in piñon property for somewhere around $35 down and $35 a month, but it's tough getting to it in the winter on the rocky roads. One Albuquerque, New Mexico, agent deals in Costilla County land. He sells it for $45 down and $45 a month. My brother bought one of his lots and set up an $800 mobile home on it.

Wherever you buy, check with the county to make sure the land taxes are paid. Don't take it for granted they are. It is possible for people to obtain land for back taxes, and you could be out your money and a place to live. (See note on tax-lien property at the end of this chapter.)

Costilla County is now zoned, as are all the surrounding counties. They are in the process of trying to hire an enforcement officer — at least to check permits — but will never be able to enforce them. There are way too many homesteaders, in too large an area, for enforcement to be effective. Existing homesteaders have already grandfathered in their land, anyhow.

Travel-Trailer Homesteading Under $5,000

Taxes in Costilla County are around $30 a year on a 5-acre tract. Many people live in trailers, shacks, or buses, and even have outhouses (why, I can't understand, when for the same cost of materials you can have a septic system — covered later in this book).

There are several artesian wells in this area that are accessible to the public. One is on Highway 160, halfway to Alamosa, and another in Blanca, in Costilla County (it used to be the town well). In addition, there are various others scattered here and there throughout the valley. These flow year-round, with good clean water, due to a large aquifer under a layer of clay beneath the valley floor. Actually, there are two aquifers — one under the clay, one over. And the clay can be shallow or deep, from 10 feet to more than 400, depending on the location.

Under pressure from water flowing underground from the mountains, a puncture of the clay layer by a well relieves pressure and yields a constant flow of water to the surface. But you can't get artesian water everywhere in the valley. For instance, at my place I can't, because the clay layer is absent this close to the mountains.

You need water available constantly. The San Luis Valley only gets just over 7 inches of precipitation a year, so water collection is not really feasible as a main supply. Trying to drain a roof or other area for water might be fine in places that get a lot of rain, but here, that would bring on thirst in a hurry. If you employ gutters for water collection, this will only be an augmentation, at best — and with few exceptions, not much of one at that.

It is quite cold here in the winter, but everybody heats with wood. I just stoke the wood stove and forget about it.

Here is the climatic data for my area, courtesy of the National Weather Service:

The San Luis Valley is called the Land of Cool Sunshine, with the sun shining more than 320 days a year. So, besides being excellent for solar power, I love it.

It rarely gets into the 90s, with 96° the highest temperature ever recorded in the valley. If it gets to 90°, you should hear the people complain.

We average fifty nights a year where the temperature falls below zero. Minus 10° is nothing. In the last four winters, I have seen it get to minus 30°, once. The coldest temperature ever recorded was an even minus 50°, but that was in the 1940s. However, don't let the cold scare you. When the sun comes up in the morning, it quickly warms things. That doesn't mean it will be 60°, but it does warm up.

With the dry climate and abundant sunshine we have, it also seems warmer than it is. There's none of that mushy wet cold like they have in Buffalo, New York.

At any rate, no matter where you locate, choose your land with care. You'll spend half your money on this purchase, and it can affect your happiness and economic situation for the future. Don't rush into anything; there's plenty out there to choose from. On the other hand, don't pass up a perfect deal, either. Trust yourself; you'll know it when you see it.

Note on Tax-Lien Properties

Before you get excited about buying tax-lien properties dirt cheap — and they are — keep in mind that you almost never get the property. The people usually pay up, and all you get is interest and your purchase money back. I have obtained a few lots this way (one adjoins my property), but you won't have clear title for nine years, because of the antiquated Sailors and Miners Act. (A person might have been away at sea or working in mines for a number of years — they picked the number nine — and not been notified that they were losing their property.) The county will instead issue you a Treasurer's Deed, not the more common Warranty Deed, and no realtor would buy the land from you, if you ever wanted to sell, unless you had first done a Quiet Title Action in court. Cost: $2,000.

It also takes at least three years of paying the back taxes before you can apply for title. Then, it's $400 to $800 to get the process moving (notification, advertising in the paper, etc.) during which time, the person can redeem at any opportunity, right up until the very day before the treasurer's deed is issued.

But it doesn't stop there. Once you receive title, it's still not clear. At any time during the nine-year period, the person the land was taken from can come back and take you to court. Once there, the burden is on you to prove that the county did everything right, legally, in taking away that person's property. Let's hope they did.

Should you get a parcel this way and sell it to somebody, if the original owner has a legitimate claim, you can then expect to be sued by the person you sold it to.

Some fun, huh? Don't mess with it, it's easier to buy land the regular way. As for my lots, I'll probably just sit on them for another seven years; I'm in no hurry. And no, I won't sell any of them (see legal mess above).

Chapter Three
Shelter

Travel trailers are the best for quick, easy dwellings because they're cheap, give all the comforts of home, and are easily transportable by ordinary vehicle. Mobile homes do give much more room, but also generally cost more, although that is not always the case. For instance, my brother paid $800 for his 10-by-40-foot mobile home, and I moved it with my ¾-ton pickup. You might say he "Mobile Homesteaded Under $5,000." But for larger mobiles, you need a semi-tractor to move them. They also require more work to set up and maintain, and when I started this, I didn't want to work on a house anymore.

For this reason, I bought a 21-foot travel trailer in good condition for $1,200. It was a 1972 Concord Traveler, with 15-inch tires, dual axles and electric brakes, which I needed. An older trailer of this size weighs approximately 4,200 pounds, and has a tongue (hitch) weight of about 425 pounds.

Naturally, because you will be living in it, the bigger the better, but don't outdo your towing vehicle. I pulled mine with a 1984 Grand Wagoneer that had a 360 V8 in it, and it was inadequate, except for engine size. I subsequently had to replace the transfer case in a small town — ka-ching! I recommend a pickup truck, preferably a ¾-ton truck with four-wheel drive. You'll need one anyway.

Besides obvious things like a bunk, you'll need the following items in your trailer:

- Kitchen — sink, stove, propane refrigerator
- Bathroom — shower, vanity, toilet with holding tank
- Water system with storage tank and hot water heater
- Propane heater or furnace (for when you're away)
- A 12-volt lighting system (most also have 110-volt lights)

Most trailers of this size have this stuff. If the one you're looking at doesn't, I wouldn't buy it, unless it's only lacking the lights. You can easily install a 12-volt lighting system, and in fact, 12-volt fluorescent lights are about four times as efficient as 12-volt incandescent bulbs. You may choose to use only a kerosene lamp in the evenings. (Don't use lamp oil; it costs much more, and I don't think it puts out as much light as kerosene.)

When you look at the trailer, make sure it's big enough and comfortable — you'll be spending a lot of time in it. Think about the floor plan. Where will you put the wood stove? I took out half of one couch and installed it next to the hot water heater.

Mine also had an apartment-sized electric refrigerator in it when I bought it — a great asset, the previous owner thought. Wrong. Initially, since I took the third couch out and built a desk for writing, I installed an icebox on one end of the desk, near the door. That was okay, but it needs ice to operate — from town, nearly every day (except in winter, when I could make my own). Also, you have no freezer, and a small propane refrigerator actually costs less to operate than the cost of ice. See the refrigeration chapter for more detailed information.

Everything in the trailer must work, or be fixable. If the propane refrigerator doesn't work, chances are you can fix it. (See the refrigeration chapter.) Dump some water into the holding tank to make sure it doesn't leak. Light all gas appliances. Check the furnace for fumes.

Setting Up

You'll want to situate your trailer in the best possible location on your land, taking advantage of access, sunlight, prevailing wind direction, and the view.

When you have that figured out, lay a couple of planks down in front of the tires (make sure they're level) and pull the trailer up onto them. This keeps the tires out of direct contact with the ground — which causes dry-rot — and also gives you a stable starting point.

Then set your trailer solidly on blocks, stands, or sections of logs. Whatever you use, be sure to put a flat piece of wood under the bases. I used the adjustable stands that came with my trailer, and put larger squares of plywood under them.

Use a level while you're tightening up the jacks or stands. Be sure and check the inside floor of the trailer, especially. You can just about get it all level from that point.

You may want to consider tie-downs for the trailer, if you live in a windy area.

Skirting

Figure 2

Skirting helps a lot. It keeps varmints and bugs out, allows you weather-proof storage under the trailer, keeps the trailer *much* warmer (especially the floor), and helps keep the plumbing and holding tank from freezing. It also looks good, and adds a sense of permanence to it all.

You can probably use a variety of things for skirting, but I recommend barn metal. I have seen fiberglass panels, wood, plywood, and even straw bales used. However, these all have drawbacks. Just look at any old carport or porch with fiber-glass panels — they're all broken or cracked. Wood's not so bad, but is a lot of work to install, and requires painting. Plywood sponges water and moisture up from the ground, de-laminating in a short time. Straw bales bring mice, bugs, and maybe even fire.

Galvanized barn metal is the best bet. It's tough, light, easy to install, never needs paint, and won't soak up moisture. It comes in convenient sizes, such as 2 feet or more in width, and 8-foot lengths.

Figure up the footage you'll need with a measuring tape, allowing for several inches overlap at each joint, including the corners. My trailer needed nine pieces — one for each end, three for each side, and an extra one that came in handy for the wheel wells, where they arch up.

You'll also need several pounds of self-tapping sheet-metal screws, a pound or so of drywall screws, several tubes of caulk, and a few 1-by-4s, which, hopefully, you'll have lying around.

Now is the time to decide whether to insulate the skirting or not. I chose not to, because of the cost of rigid Styrofoam — about $27 a sheet. Regular fiberglass batt installation is much cheaper, but I thought it might be a haven for bugs, so I passed on it. However, if you think you need it, buy it. If I had it to do over again, I'd probably do it. You'll need to figure out how to hang, nail, wire, or brace it into place, and probably any of these would do.

Now before you start the skirting, find the best location for access panels. You'll need at least one of these, and preferably two. This panel will lap over and screw onto a regular skirting panel on each end.

Figure how deep your skirting will be into the ground, and dig a narrow trench all the way around the trailer. Now start installing the barn metal, working from a corner.

You want to lap up the trailer, at least to the trim at the bottom. Make sure the edge of the sheet lies against the trailer, making a nice seal. That is, the wave of the corrugation should curve into the trailer. I lapped up two corrugations on the trailer and screwed directly into the plastic trim.

At the ends of the panels, cut a piece of 1-by-4 and attach it behind where the joint will be. Obviously, you can't lap the trailer with this, so cut it short enough to fit underneath it — it doesn't have to attach to the RV.

Starting at the end of one side of the trailer, screw the first panel onto the trim, with sheet-metal screws. You will need to run both ends of both sides of the skirting slightly past the ends of the trailer, to make the corners. Then, using drywall screws, attach the 1-by-4 to the sheet. You may want to "back up" the piece of wood to make it easier to screw. If you use your hand, make sure it's out of the way of where the screw will come through. Running a screw into your hand is quite painful, I can assure you. It's just as well to hold another board or a large hammer behind it.

Now, if you are insulating, install whatever kind you are using behind the first piece of skirting. But regardless of whether you insulate or not, backfill this section of trench with dirt.

Screw the next panel in place, using one self-tapper at the joint. Line up the other end of the second sheet for height, and screw the panel to the trim. Put the remaining screws into the joint (they'll run through the first sheet and into the 1-by-4). Insulate or backfill, or both, with dirt.

At this point, you're probably up to where your access panel will be. Skipping that space, cut a sheet to complete the run, bearing in mind the distance to go past the corner and to lap under the access panel. Install this sheet. Again, insulate or backfill behind it.

Cut your access panel to size and install it with the self-tappers. (Note: If you are insulating, you must somehow attach the material to the back of the sheet.)

Also shear and install a piece to cover the wheel wells, lapping the trim and the panel below it. There's not much you can do about the exposed spaces behind the corrugations on the ends of this little panel except caulk them.

One side is now complete. Do the other side in the same manner.

For the ends, you'll cut one sheet to fit between both sides. This means you'll cut the waves of the corrugations on both ends of this panel. After measuring for the sheet, do this with the panel lying down, by standing a cut-off piece on edge, directly on the sheet where the corner will be. Trace the general outline of the corrugations with a magic marker, and cut them with tin snips. You don't have to be perfect, you'll caulk this joint anyhow. If you don't want to follow the curve exactly — and you don't need to — you can simply cut the corrugations out in small triangles.

On the front of the trailer, you'll probably have to cut around the frame, gas line, and maybe some wiring. Draw your cutouts or holes with the magic marker, then simply cut down to the center of each from the top of the sheet, and make your cutouts. This leaves as much of the sheet in place as possible, yet still allows for fairly easy installation — simply pull out one side of the metal at the cut and slide the sheet up around the obstruction.

Install a 1-by-4 at the corners, onto the end panel of the skirting along the sides of the trailer. Maneuver the sheet into place — this one is perhaps the most difficult — and screw through the panel into the edge of the 1-by-4.

Do the same thing with the rear panel on the trailer. You probably won't need any cutouts at this end. However, the other consideration here is the bumper. Depending on your trailer, you may want to cut around and install it under the bumper, directly to the trailer. On mine, the bumper was a square tube projecting out from the trailer, and I used it as a surface to screw into, bending the sheet over the top of the bumper and securing it with self-tappers. Depending on the thickness of the metal, you may have to drill a hole in the bumper first, just slightly smaller than the self-tapper. Otherwise, you'll snap a bunch of screws off.

Use a 1-by-4 or 2-by-4 in the corners, under the bumper. Screw the panel into place.

Now, caulk the corner joints, all gaps that need it, and any projections coming through the skirting, such as the frame on the front. Don't caulk the access panels.

The metal fit so well against my trailer that I didn't need to caulk it where the horizontal top line of the skirting curves into the trailer siding. But if you need to, do it.

Also cut a small access panel — just big enough to get your hand through — where the holding tank valve is. Put a piece over this and screw it on.

Fill dirt against the skirting and you're in business.

Isn't it nice to have a warm floor?

Chapter Four
The Septic System

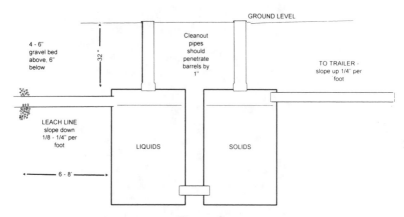

Figure 3
Septic system layout.

You can build an inexpensive, fully functional septic system for under $100 if you can get the rock free or cheap.

My system cost me a total of $70, with the PVC piping as the major expense.

This is a very simple system, but requires the most output of physical labor to install if you dig it by hand. I dug mine with a shovel, and it took me more than a week on the excavation alone. If you have any neighbors with a backhoe, lucky you.

Because your trailer's plumbing is set up the same as in a regular house — for the most part — you do not need to install any vents in the septic system itself. If you look on the top of the trailer, you will see at least one plumbing vent sticking up, and more likely two. Your septic tanks will vent directly through these, as will your holding tank.

This system works with two barrels, one for solids, and one for liquids. The solids drop into the first barrel, where they decompose. The liquids flow into the second barrel, and out the leach line.

Figure 4
Plastic barrels are preferred for the septic system
— metal ones will rust and leak.

For the tanks themselves, you will need two plastic barrels, 55-gallon size. You can get them from a variety of places, such as stores, factories, or crop dusters, but I purchased mine from a local honey farm. The walls are ¼-inch thick. These are standard sized drums, with the usual two openings in the top. Lids are needed for the openings, as these will be sealed.

My barrels were $5 each, and simply needed to be washed out. Although they're going to contain sewage, I washed mine out, anyway. I want those bacteria down there eating waste, not making fruit salad.

Do not use metal barrels, as these will quickly rust out and leak. Your system will be destroyed, and you'll be digging up a dirty mess to install plastic barrels.

For the sewer line itself, from the trailer to the tanks, use standard 4-inch PVC plumbing sewer pipe. PVC comes in several grades, but ask for the thin-walled stuff, as the thick-walled is more expensive, and not needed. This comes in 10-foot sections, and one end is flared to accept the regular end of the next section of pipe. Be sure to buy PVC cement to glue the joints together. Chances are, the store owner will also try to sell you primer, which is applied before the glue, but this is unnecessary, and most plumbers don't bother with it.

From the tanks outward, you need a leach line, also of 4-inch PVC pipe, but perforated just for this purpose. This pipe is available with the holes already drilled, but if they happen to be out of stock, simply buy the solid pipe and drill the holes yourself. It costs about the same for both pipes, so try to buy the pre-drilled kind. The holes are generally about a ½-inch in diameter, spaced every 12 inches or so, and are drilled so as to be on both sides of the lower third of the pipe when installed.

You will need two 90-degree elbows. You also need a 3-inch to 4-inch adapter fitting, and two caps.

The drums are joined together about 4 to 5 inches up from the bottom with a section of solid 4-inch pipe, about one foot long. (See Figures 5 and 6.)

Note: Some people who read the first edition of this book were concerned that this joining pipe may be too low, and thereby get plugged with sludge. But I have been on my original septic for four years now, and haven't had a single problem with it. Not one. Indeed, a year after I did mine, I installed another system for my brother — in exactly the same fashion

— and it also functions perfectly, despite the fact that the only bacteria he puts in it is an occasional dead mouse.

I did know one person who put a second joining pipe in his barrels, up near the top, but I don't think that's a good idea. I believe it would allow some of the solids or paper to float into the second barrel — possibly even the leach line — and may cause a backup or slowdown of the system. And there's also the consideration of more penetrations in the barrels. More holes could mean more chance of leakage, something you want to stay away from.

Of course, the other option would be to simply raise the single joining pipe up higher, say, closer to halfway up the barrels. If you want a second pipe, that's up to you. But don't put it more than halfway up, if at all.

At any rate, here's how to install the joining pipe:

Using the *inside* diameter of a small section of pipe (cut a 2-inch piece off one of the longer sections if you don't have a short piece lying around), trace the circle onto the barrel with a pencil or pen. Be sure it's a round circle — don't crush the pipe with your hands as you trace it, or you'll have an ellipse instead of a circle, and it may leak.

Drill a hole near the edge of the inside of your circle with a large standard drill bit or paddle bit. The hole needs to be large enough to accommodate the blade of your jigsaw. Cut your holes out, being careful to stay either inside of or right on your traced lines. A jigsaw is best turned in a circle by pivoting the saw on the blade, that is, by turning the rear of the saw, not by trying to move the blade over with the pressure of your hand.

After the cut is finished, remove the cutouts from the barrels as they could cover or plug one of the lines if they fell in. Now trim up the cuts with your wood rasp, being careful not to take too much out.

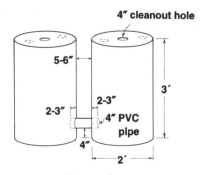

Figure 5
Joining septic barrels.

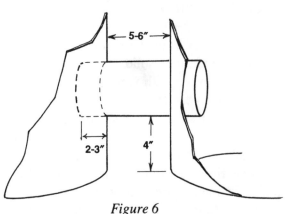

Figure 6
You want a tight fit when you join your barrels; the pipe will slide
in easier when you lubricate the openings with caulk.

Take your 1-foot section of 4-inch pipe and try to shove it forcefully into the hole of one of the barrels. It probably won't go at first try, and you'll need to continue filing and trying until you can force the pipe in. You want a tight fit, so as not to leak. The pipe will slide in easier when you caulk the holes, which will provide lubrication.

When you can do this with both barrels, apply silicone to the edges of one of the holes. Also apply it to one end of your 1-foot section of pipe, about 3 inches from the end. Run two good-sized continuous beads of caulk around the pipe, about ¼ inch apart. Now, laying the barrel on its side, push the pipe into the hole until you make contact with the second bead of silicone. Then leave it.

Caulk the hole in the second barrel and the end of the pipe sticking out of the first barrel. This connection will be harder to make. When I did it, it was accompanied by some mild cussing. The problem is, you don't have much room to work between the two barrels. You must grip the connecting pipe itself to shove it into the second barrel; you cannot simply line it up and shove on the first. That would only push the pipe farther into the first drum. I recommend placing the second barrel against something solid, in an upright position, and working the pipe into it with your hands. Again, push it in until you make contact with the second bead of silicone.

The pipe should stick into each barrel by several inches. Look down through the openings in the tops to make sure this is so. It doesn't have to be perfect, and if it sticks into one barrel farther than the other, don't worry about it. You should end up with about 5 inches or so between the barrels.

At this point, find the center of the tops of the barrels, and trace the *outside* of a 2-inch section of pipe onto the tops of the barrels. These will be the clean-outs.

Cut these out, being careful again to retrieve the cutouts. I find it easier to drill a second hole directly in the center of the circle, and stick a finger in this hole when I am finishing my cut. This keeps it from dropping into the barrel. Should it fall in anyhow, simply pound a nail into the end of a stick and bend it over like a hook. Use this to fish it out. Now tape over these holes with duct tape.

Next, silicone the existing threaded holes in the tops of the barrels, and install the caps tightly. Go over the edges with silicone for a good seal.

Now put a lot of silicone around the connecting pipe at the bottom of the barrels for an extra-strong seal. This is perhaps the most important connection in the system.

When you install your septic, you should sink your system deep enough to prevent it from freezing. I have 32 inches of dirt over the tops of my barrels, and the lines are just slightly lower than that. Measure the height of your barrels, add 32 inches, and start digging. This is the hardest part, believe me.

You'll also need to dig trenches for the sewer and leach lines. The sewer line needs to maintain a constant slope to the septic tank.

You are now ready to place the barrels in the hole. Because they are so light, just grab them by the edge of the tops and lower them into the hole. While moving them, try to be careful not to twist or move the barrels around in reference to each other — you want that good seal.

Position the barrels in the center of your hole, as level as the eye allows, and fill in around them with a little dirt, maybe up a foot or so, so the barrels will not move. Don't compact the fill at this point; this will allow for the barrels to expand when they fill with waste.

Now, recheck the depth of your trenches for the sewer line to the trailer and the leach line. *Everything* now should work from the height of your barrels. Should you find that your trenches are not deep enough, *do not* attempt to raise the barrels and allow dirt to fill in underneath. If you do this, they will settle later, possibly crushing the lines in and out, giving you a big headache, and probably another backache when you have to dig up and fix everything. Work from the setting of the barrels, by either filling in or digging more out of your trenches. If you should need to fill your sewer line trench from the trailer, be sure to compact it by walking over the fill until it's hard-packed. The slope of the sewer line must be maintained.

The next step is to install the solid sewer line to your trailer.

Cut another hole in your first (solids) barrel, the one closest to your trailer. Make this cut up as high as you can on the side of the barrel, just under where the barrel rounds over into the top. You will be following the same procedure with this hole as you did with the one-foot connecting pipe between the barrels. That is, trace the inside, file, silicone, and shove it in several inches.

Make sure this line slopes ¼-inch to the foot, *uphill* to the trailer. This is very important. Less than ¼-inch doesn't allow the solids to slide downhill. More than ¼-inch generally allows the liquids to out-pace the solids — the solids get stuck on the bottom of the pipe, clogging the sewer line.

Use a level on this. An easy trick to make sure you're getting the right slope is to tape a block of wood of the appropriate thickness on one end of your level. If you're using a 4-foot level, a 1-inch block would be correct (¼-inch to the foot). A 2-foot level would require a ½-inch block.

You can now lay the level directly on top of the sewer pipe, and when it reads level, you're right on target.

You want as straight a line from the tank to the trailer as possible. You may need a few elbows; ideally, there will be only two, one at the trailer connection to send the waste downward, and the other directly beneath it, underground, to direct the waste towards the tank.

You may want to install a clean-out in your sewer line, where the line plunges directly downward after turning down from the trailer, just in case you ever need to snake it.

Most trailers use a 3-inch PVC waste pipe, and because we are working with 4-inch pipe, this is where the 3- to 4-inch adapter fitting comes in. The trailer's waste pipe usually has two prongs on it to facilitate the connection of the flexible RV sewer pipe. Make sure your adapter will fit the trailer plumbing, and then simply saw the prongs off with a hacksaw. File smooth, and make your connection.

A special consideration here is the trailer's holding tank. Usually, the holding tank holds only toilet waste, and the sinks and shower lines connect to the waste pipe *after* the holding tank valve, allowing them to flow freely at all times.

I recommend leaving the system intact. It is much easier than cutting through the bottom of the trailer and holding tank and then trying to rig a connection to the toilet. Also, RV toilets don't send much water down the tubes when they flush, relying instead on the liquid waste that accumulates in the holding tank to flush the solids when the valve is pulled. Since the toilet uses so little water, it's usually not sufficient to send the solids to the other end of the holding tank, where the outlet is. RV toilets usually just drop the bowl's contents straight down into the holding tank.

I think putting toilet waste directly into the sewer line without a water medium to send the solids on their way will clog your sewer line *muy pronto*.

For these reasons, I recommend leaving the system intact and using the holding tank. Every other day or so, simply pull the valve and send the sewage on its way. This will necessitate a small access panel in the trailer skirting to reach the valve. Once a week, after emptying the tank, I send 3 or 4 gallons of water from a jug down the toilet, all at once and in a hurry, to make sure everything reaches the septic and the lines stay clear.

However, in extremely cold weather, you may want to leave the valve open, so your pipe doesn't freeze solid and burst. In that case, you may want to send a gallon or two down the toilet at the end of the day. But the trailer skirting does wonders for keeping the plumbing warm. I only leave my valve open when the night time temperature will be around zero or below.

Figure 7
Installing the leach line for the septic system.

From your liquids barrel, you need a leach line outward, to carry the liquids away to where they'll be absorbed into the ground.

You should make your hole in this drum several inches lower than the inlet hole (the sewer line from the trailer) in the solids barrel. This will allow the sewage to fall into the septic tank, keeping the level of the tanks lower than the inlet line, so that nothing lays in the sewer line, creating a clog or blockage. I made mine 2½ inches lower. You should make this connection in the same way as the others — trace, cut, file, caulk, and shove it in.

The perforated line should start about 8 feet out from the tanks, so the first section of pipe should be solid. You don't want the liquids to seep around the tanks, possibly settling them and destroying the integrity of your system.

The leach line also needs to be sloped, and I used the same ¼-inch to the foot, here. It can, however, be slightly less than that, but ⅛-inch per foot is the minimum. To be safe, go ¼-inch.

You only need one line out, as opposed to the multiple lines popularly in use in larger home systems. It should be a straight line — no elbows are required.

The length of your line can vary, depending on your soil conditions and the wetness of the area you live in. In my area, we get just over 7 inches of precipitation a year, and the soil is dry and sandy. My line is 35 feet of perforated pipe, and 8 feet of solid. If you get a lot of rain, I'd suggest making your line a little longer.

Your trench should be about 2 feet wide, and approximately 6 inches deeper than where the pipe will actually be sitting, to allow for rock under it. You will need to slope the ditch, and the pipe. At the end of your trench, dig it wider and deeper, making a pit you can fill with gravel.

Figure 8
You will need to slope the ditch and the pipe. Dig the end deeper and wider, and make a pit to fill with gravel.

The rock should be gravel-sized or larger, and you will need about three pickup loads of it. I used red volcanic rock — real light stuff — from a local aggregate company, which didn't even sell it anymore. There were some piles lying around, and upon asking — *and* spending a few extra minutes talking with the man in charge — they gave it to me for free. They even put one load in my truck with a front-end loader. It pays to be friendly and to live near a small town.

Fill the ditch by eye to the approximate level of the bottom of the pipe. Then, start your installation, using the level. The gravel is easy to work with, and can be scraped or kicked around as needed for the proper slope. The perforations, of course, are to be installed towards the bottom of the ditch. I also drilled some ¼-inch holes along the bottom of my pipes, spaced 2 feet apart on the first section, 16 inches on the next, and 1 foot on the third piece. On my last 5-foot section, at the pit, I drilled holes every few inches.

There are to be *no holes* in the top of the pipes, as this will allow sand and dirt into the pipes, plugging them.

Figure 9
The end of the leach line.

At the end of your leach line, insert a small coffee can directly into the end of the pipe and run a few screws through it to seal the line. You're only keeping gravel out, so it isn't necessary to make a water-tight seal. One person I knew just put an elbow at the end, turned down into the pit, but I like the coffee can.

When the entire line is in place, go ahead and fill the ditch with gravel, covering the top with 6 inches, if you can.

Then, cover the gravel with plastic or building paper. Some people have used a thick layer of straw, but I'm against this. Straw is organic and may decompose. Plastic, as the saying goes, never goes away. But whatever you use, this is important to do, because if you don't cover the gravel, dirt and sand will settle down through it, and you guessed it — clog the line. That would be a catastrophe, and you'd be digging again. I used two layers of clear plastic, the kind you put over windows in the winter. Cost: about $2.50.

When this is done, backfill the trench completely.

Next, you want to install clean-outs in the tops of the barrels, where you already have the holes cut and duct-taped. These will be solid 4-inch PVC pipes, running straight up to ground level.

These will need to be self-supporting, and so you must use a straight connection, or the flared end of a pipe. In either case, you'll need to cut two pieces several inches long, and insert them in the flared ends or connections. This extra width, or "collar," is what holds the pipes up.

Silicone the connections, and brace the pipes in place by wiring them to sticks jammed sideways against the sides of the excavation, but allow them to float, as the tops of the barrels are bound to sag a little under the weight of the soil when you fill over them and you don't want dirt leaking into your tanks. Seal around the connections again, and don't spare the caulking here.

At ground level, slip the PVC caps over the pipes, without sealant.

Now, finish your backfill of the entire excavation.

Congratulations! You are now in business.

Figure 10
The ideal septic system has as straight a line
as possible from the tank to the trailer.

I recommend backfilling the tanks as the barrels fill, so they are completely expanded when you fill in the dirt. I didn't compact any of the fill around my tanks, to allow for this.

I also recommend inserting bacteria into the tanks to get the system functioning. One person with a new full-sized tank threw in a road-killed rabbit to start the bacteria process. To start with, I put some bacteria down the clean-out of the solids tank. However, you can also simply flush this product down the toilet, or put it in your sink drain. Generally, a septic system promotes its own bacteria, but because this is a small system, I recommend adding it at regular intervals.

A product such as RID-X will do the job, and costs about $5 a box at a hardware store. A small box should last you for many months. I add it about every ten days, about two table-spoons at a time.

A system like this takes about two weeks to install, but beats an outhouse any day, especially the cold ones. And because going to the bathroom at night doesn't involve shoes and a flashlight, well, you know the rest....

Happy flushing.

A few notes on using this system:

1: *Do not* pour *any* kitchen grease down the sink, or any-where else, for that matter. Be very careful about this. Grease does not decompose, despite the claims on bacteria boxes. It's carried on the water and builds up in your system the same as it does when you pour it in an old jar. And that's exactly the way it will look when you have to cut your pipes apart, look-ing for the blockage when your pipes back up. My neighbor — the one who showed me how to make this system (and warned me about the grease) — had to do this in the middle of winter. He was so mad at his wife that he actually shot the pipe apart under his trailer. Ever see those programs on PBS about core-drilling the ice in Antarctica? That's how the grease looked coming out of there, in cores. Knowing his sep-tic was completely wasted, he was forced to install a new one.

After cooking, if there's not a lot of grease in the pan, I pour it right on the junk mail in the garbage can. (Yes, even out here you still get junk mail.) When you burn your trash, it goes up in smoke. If there's a lot, I put it in the old grease-jar, which still gets burned. Then I wipe the pans out with paper towels.

2: No antibacterial soaps for your dishes or your hands, please. You need those bacteria down there doing their job, let's not kill them off.

3: See Chapter Five, Water, the Cistern. Don't go overboard with the occasional adding of chlorine bleach. The idea is to kill any bacteria in the water storage tank, not the septic. In fact, after I add bleach to the cistern, two days later I add an extra helping of RID-X to the septic, just to be sure.

4: Do not flush any feminine hygiene products, male contraceptive devices, chewing gum, dental floss, or paper down the toilet (toilet paper excepted, and don't go overboard with that, either). This is a septic system for human waste. Some kitchen waste is acceptable: a few food particles or sour milk, for instance. But NO GREASE!

There are other alternatives to this septic system, but to tell you the truth, I don't think much of them. I'll put my money on a real, contained septic system any day. It's a well-proven design.

Chapter Five
Water

You will need a year-round, non-freezing, clean and free supply of water, and it must be close, or at least on your way to town. Perhaps a neighbor with a well would be willing to let you get it there. Or, if you work, you can probably just bring it home with you. Ask permission first, though. Then, when people ask where you get your water, you can tell them you've got "city water." But, of course, if you can afford a well, that is the most desirable way to go.

Assuming you can't, you will need to haul water to your homestead, unless you happen to have a stream running through your property. Land with streams, however, is non-existent in the price range we are targeting. Should you be able to get such a piece, count your blessings, you are one of the chosen few.

Barring this, prepare to haul water.

It's not that much of a bother, and since you will have a small storage system, you will probably only have to do this once every week or so, depending on how much you can haul and store, and how well you conserve water.

Water conservation is necessary, but I don't find it restrictive. No, I don't wash my truck here at home, and I do laundry in town (I'm there anyway for groceries and other things), but I still take a shower, flush my toilet at every use, and do dishes every day.

The Trailer

A trailer for our purposes already has a water system in place — this is essential.

It must have a bathroom with toilet, sink, and shower, and also a kitchen sink. It also must have an existing water tank inside the structure, because we'll be pressurizing that system.

You have two choices for pressurization: a water pump or an air pump.

A 12-volt RV on-demand water pump is sure nice, but costs two or three times what an air pump does. These are available from RV dealers for under $100, but you can get one from J.C. Whitney for about $60. Different pumps generate and maintain different amounts of pressure. The pump number 74VY8421A comes on at 20 psi and off at 35; pump number 81VY2262W comes on at 13 psi and off at 18. The first draws 3 amps, and the second, 4½. These pumps are sure nice, and water pressure is available on demand, but I have my reservations about them, besides the amount of power they use.

Travel trailers aren't really designed for winter living conditions. They're mostly summer vacation shelters, but we can get around that. Consequently, water pipes in them tend to run in odd-ball, out of the way places, and during extremely cold weather (below zero) I have had them sometimes freeze in certain locations. Although I took care of that by exposing lines and leaving cabinet doors open at night, I wouldn't want to take a chance on a pipe bursting — with pressurized water behind it. Pipes that are filled with water but not pressurized don't burst when they freeze, at least that's my experience, and I had them freeze a lot before I figured out what to do about it.

If you use a water pump, put a switch on it, and turn it off every night and every time you leave. You probably won't have to worry, except for the times you forget to switch it off.

What I used was an old style 12-volt air pump I obtained inexpensively. It has a rubber hose on it with an end piece that is threaded to screw onto an automotive tire valve stem, for inflating tires. My trailer was set up for such a pump in the outside storage compartment at the rear, and so I tried it. It worked fine.

I hooked it up to the batteries, with a switch in the line (on the bathroom wall) and it worked fine until the cold weather really set in. The pressure line ran under the trailer, and condensation in the line would freeze up — the result: no water.

So I removed it from there, and with the help of a few pipe fittings, installed it where a plug had been in the filler line above the water tank. The air valve itself is a one-way valve, otherwise water might back up into the pump. The pump is screwed to a board that sits on the floor right next to the water tank. No freeze-ups, and all this is hidden under one of the couches.

You can buy these emergency air pumps from Kmart or just about any big department store for under $30, sometimes half that. They have 12-volt cigarette lighter plug-ins on them, but you simply cut that off and wire it for a wall plug. Be careful with these pumps; don't let them run too long. Some have up to 200 psi capacity, and you don't need anywhere near that much. Mine only puts out about 25 psi, and works just fine.

I used a regular light switch for the pump, mounted on the bathroom wall within easy reach while in the shower. You always know when the pump is running, because you can hear it operating. It's impossible to walk away and forget about it. I find that my water system loses pressure by itself after about thirty minutes, so I don't worry about bursting the pipes.

The Cistern

Figure 11
Use only clean, chemical-free plastic drums
for your water cisterns.

I first started by using 6-gallon water jugs from Wal-Mart, two at a time, and pouring the water directly into my trailer's water tank. But it gets to be a pain in the neck going for water every day. When I bought a third jug, that helped, as I could go every other day.

But it became a chore to go all the time, besides the gasoline I used. So I came up with an idea for a small cistern. Here's how it works:

Get three more plastic barrels, a 10-foot section of 3-inch inside diameter PVC pipe (check your barrels first to see if this is the right size for your needs), two 45-degree elbows, a cap, and a tube of silicone. Also buy 10 feet of $3/8$-inch plastic water line, and a 12-volt submersible RV water pump. I got mine from J.C. Whitney, part number 14VY4805B. This pump is $18.95, and is only 4½ inches long by 1½ inch in diameter, and will fit easily through the hole in the barrel.

Dig a 6-foot hole under your trailer, directly under the water tank, and put a barrel in this hole. Place it so one of the holes in the top of the drum is directly underneath where your water line will come down from the trailer.

Drill a ⅝-inch or bigger hole in the trailer floor for the water line and wiring.

Pipe straight up to the hole in the floor of the trailer with the PVC. This pipe should fit directly over the flange for one of the two threaded holes in the top of the barrel. You may need to file some of the flange off with a wood rasp. Make a tight fit. Now remove the pipe.

Connect the wiring and water line to the pump, and drop it into the barrel. Make sure it's near the bottom. I held mine up about an inch, in case any sediment collects on the bottom of the barrel. Heavily silicone the flange.

Now run the water line and pump wiring through the PVC and up through the hole in the trailer floor. Silicone and install the PVC pipe into place. This is somewhat difficult, and you may find you need a small gap between the trailer and the pipe. Silicone or otherwise seal off where the pipe meets the bottom of the trailer.

Next, install the filler pipe, again using a lot of silicone. Come up with about a 1-foot piece and glue an elbow on it. Place the next straight section into the elbow, coming out far enough that your filler tube will be outside the trailer. Now is a good time to wire this pipe into place temporarily. Put on the next elbow, and pipe up to however high you want it. My cap is 8 inches above ground.

You can now fill the cistern and backfill the barrel.

The next step is to make the connection of the water line to the trailer water tank. You'll need a valve of some kind; I used a regular household type water valve, the kind you turn.

Travel-Trailer Homesteading Under $5,000

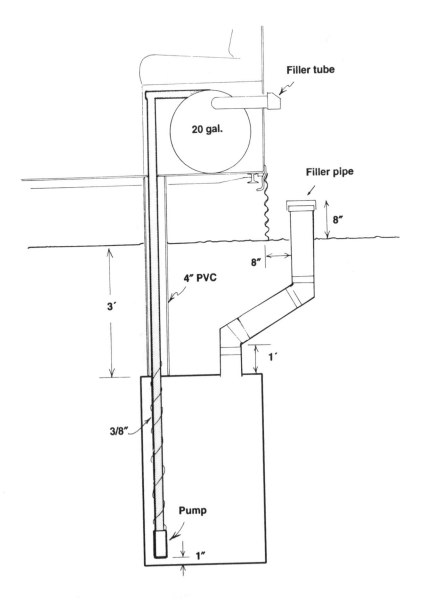

*Figure 12
Water system layout.*

You'll need various fittings to accomplish this, and a small hose clamp. Use whatever works easiest and best for you. My water tank already had two plugs on it, attached to piping on the top of the tank, at the opposite end from the external filler tube. However you do it, you need the water to fill from the top of the tank, so you can hear how full it's getting, and also so you don't strain that little pump too hard.

Wire the pump to the switch, silicone around the lines coming through the floor, and presto!

To fill the trailer's water tank, open the valve you installed, and remove the cap on the outside of the trailer — the water tank's filler tube. This *must* be removed during filling. It allows you to hear how full the tank is getting, but most importantly, allows the tank to fill. This little pump doesn't have the power to fill the tank without venting — which effectively pressurizes the tank. And while it's a good pump, it's not strong enough for that. You'll soon know when the tank is full, generally when it stops making noise — when you no longer hear the sound of falling water. But pay close attention when filling. Don't run the pump dry; that's bad for it.

After the tank is full, screw the cap back on outside, and close the valve. That's all there is to it. The pump is self-draining — you'll hear it when you shut it off — and so you don't have to worry about the line freezing.

Don't forget about closing the valve. If you do, you'll notice when you throw your pressurizing switch that it takes a long time to get water — if it comes at all. That's because you're inadvertently trying to pressurize the cistern along with the water tank.

I haul water a barrel at a time in the winter, and simply use a short garden hose to siphon the water from the barrel, as it sits in the back of my truck, down into the cistern. When it's warmer, I get two barrels at a time. Siphon one into the cistern, and put that empty barrel on the ground. Then siphon the other barrel into the empty one. When the cistern goes dry, you simply siphon your extra barrel down into it.

I do conserve water, but with the exception of a Navy shower, I'm not totally miserly. A cistern-full (one barrel) lasts me a whole week.

> A note on barrels: Use only clean, chemical-free drums. Don't use ones you get from a crop-duster or factory. While those might be fine for a septic system, you don't want to poison yourself once you've finally gotten your freedom.

If your water needs are greater, or if you house more people, it might be possible to join two barrels together, although I'm not keen on the idea. In any event, I don't recommend joining them the way we joined the septic barrels. They do make PVC fittings for this purpose, but they have a seal and a plastic nut that needs to be tightened from the inside. There's no way you can get into the barrel to do this, unless you cut a hole in the top and then seal it up, so you'd have to leave them off, and make your hole real tight so you could thread the fitting in, and silicone it well. In my way of thinking, the fewer holes in the cistern, the better.

If you need more storage, an easier way would be to get your hands on a bigger barrel. I upgraded my cistern by trading an old junk car somebody gave me for a 165-gallon plastic container that has the shape of a giant, old-fashioned milk can. I simply plumbed it the same way, using the same pump, and it works great.

No matter what you use for a cistern, every once in a while you should add a few drops of chlorine to the tank to combat any bacteria that might build up. The easiest way is to use plain old chlorine bleach, like Clorox, or a generic. This is quite safe, and will not affect the drinkability of your water, provided you don't put too much in. It doesn't take much: A quarter teaspoon purifies about 500 gallons, so just add a few drops now and then. You'll know when it's time to do this: The water will have just the slightest odor to it. But don't add too much; you don't want to kill the bacteria in your septic system, which is where most of the water ends up.

An interesting side note on water: A homesteading friend I met through the first edition of this book wrote to tell me about his water supply. He was fortunate enough to buy land 6 miles from a spring that sits higher than the road. He got the consent of the owner to bury a 200-gallon tank in the little hillside above the road. The tank is now plumbed and working. To fill his truck tank, he just backs his truck underneath the pipe and turns on the valve.

Chapter Six
Power

Some power is needed, and depending on your needs, there are several alternatives.

Power will be used for lights, the water-pressure pump, communications reception (radio and television), battery charging, and any other needs you may have, such as electric typewriters or the like.

I'm not talking about curling irons, blow-dryers, can openers, electric motors, or electric heaters. A hand can opener works just fine, and the others take so much energy as not to be practical. Anything that produces heat by electricity is out of the question, and so are large electric motors. If you absolutely must have a toaster, get a campfire version and put it on your stove.

There are several sources of cheaply obtained power, and a generator stands out foremost, at least at first. It's the cheapest and easiest to use, but won't last forever.

Next is solar power, followed by wind power.

There still remain several others, such as hydroelectricity, but that entails that ever-elusive and highly expensive stream.

Generators

Figure 13
The Honda EX650 generator produces 650 watts of power.

Small generators are portable, easy to come by, very quiet, and only sip gasoline. I use a Honda EX650, which produces 650 watts of power. It also includes a built-in 12-volt battery charger that produces an output of 8.7 amps. Before I had solar, I'd charge my batteries while watching the evening news on the 110-volt side of the generator.

I highly recommend purchasing one with this charging feature, since you will use batteries. You'll need it for cloudy days when your solar panels aren't charging much. Also, it can start your truck should the battery fail.

Mine runs approximately six hours on a ½-gallon of gasoline. That's not much fuel.

Unless you watch TV all day, however, the generator will get its most use when you are first setting up your homestead, running drills and other tools. With solar, the generator is only occasionally used.

Since this will initially be your only power source, take good care of it. Change the oil religiously, ground the unit when you're using it, and keep it stored indoors.

Solar Power

Figure 14
The solar panel requires no fuel, oil changes,
and starts upon sunrise, not by pulling a cord.

This is an excellent way to go, especially in areas that receive a lot of sunshine, such as where I live.

There are no moving parts to wear out, and once the system is in place, you are set. Of course, you need batteries to store the electricity produced, a regulator to make charging automatic, and an inverter to convert the power into 110 volts. This system requires no weekly expenditure for fuel, no oil changes, and is started by the sunrise, not by pulling a cord. It's also very quiet, something I've come to appreciate.

Solar panels (sometimes referred to as PV or photovoltaic panels), produce power in 12 volts DC (direct current). And because electricity cannot be stored in 110 volts AC (alternating current), it needs to be stored in batteries.

Special batteries are made just for solar systems, but they are expensive. Some people use big, old telephone company batteries, some use golf cart batteries, and some use regular car batteries. However, deep-cycle RV batteries work just fine, and for the amount of electricity I use, they were the best purchase. After all, this is an RV; they are made for exactly this purpose.

You need deep-cycle batteries because you can draw them down a long way, therefore, they last longer than car batteries. They also take longer to charge, but with all-day solar charging, this is not a problem.

My solar power setup cost a total of $692, and consists of a set of four 1-foot-by-4-foot panels, a regulator, four batteries, and a power inverter.

The panels were $215 delivered, and I purchased them from Abraham Solar (124 Creekside Place, Pagosa Springs, Colorado 81147. Phone: (800) 222-7242 or (970) 731-4675). I highly recommend Mick Abraham as a reputable dealer, no matter where you homestead. He has been in business for fifteen years, and has an incredible 100-page catalog ($4) of reasonably priced solar products that ship directly to your door. This *Alternative Energy Catalog and Guide* is *well* worth the money, as it also contains products such as refrigerators, appliances, pumps, and lights. In addition, it has useful charts and schematics, and browsing through it you'll find many ideas for setting up your homestead.

Call on the toll-free number to order the catalog or merchandise. Call Mick on your dime for questions or advice, he'll be happy to chat with you.

The panels I bought were used, but worked very well, and carried a one-year guarantee. I am still using them four years later without a single problem. These panels are rated at 17.5 volts, 87 watts, and charge at 5 amps. Mine perform better than this, due to the high altitude and direct sunshine where I live.

These panels were a bargain, and come on the market intermittently. The dealers purchased them from large solar projects throughout the nation that were either shutting down or replacing their panels. Abraham Solar tells me these particular panels are getting hard to come by, but there are plenty of other kinds to choose from. Keep up with listings in some of the rural/country/self-sufficiency publications.

I also purchased the regulator from Abraham. Those of you who read the first edition will note that I first used a switch, instead. But human beings can be quite forgetful about switches, and leave them on or off. Either one causes a problem. Forget to turn it on, and your batteries stay low. Forget to turn it off, and your batteries boil, ruining them and possibly causing a fire. Besides, you have to be there to throw the switch, and if you're off cutting wood, you can't leave it on.

So I bought a regulator. It's a Trace model C30A+, costs $67, and can handle 15 amps, or three sets of these panels. A regulator makes the charging completely automatic, by clicking on or off when the voltage gets too high or too low. Buy one of these little units and you'll never have to worry about switches again.

For batteries, it's best to purchase them locally, as they weigh so much that it's not cost-effective to ship them. I have four of the largest marine/RV batteries that Western Auto carried. They cost $260. These can also be purchased at Kmart or Wal-Mart, and many auto parts stores.

Installation

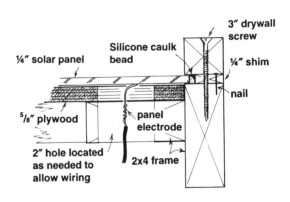

Figure 15
Solar-panel installation at the end of a platform.

Since direct sunlight produces the most power, some people mount their solar panels on a movable platform and simply push it to face the sun several times during the day. The east in the morning, south at noon, and towards the west in the evening. I don't need that much power, and elected to mount mine stationary, facing the south.

For the platform, I bought a 4-foot-by-8-foot sheet of exterior grade (CDX) ⅝-inch plywood, six 2-by-4-by-8s, a large handful of 3-inch drywall screws, another of 1½-inch screws, two tubes of silicone, and a gallon of white paint to make the platform match my trailer. This material cost $70.

I screwed 2-by-4s flat to the back of the platform, with the exception of the top one, which I glued and screwed to the trailer. With the help of my neighbor, I then hoisted the platform into position, screwed down through the plywood into that top 2-by-4, and then screwed the supporting legs to the trailer.

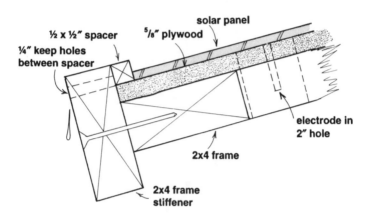

Figure 16
Be sure to paint the platform well, because
too much rain will delaminate the plywood.

After adding blocks to the ends, and another 2-by-4 for a lip at the bottom (which also helps keep the platform from sagging), I laid out the platform for panels.

This platform is big enough to allow for a second set of panels, if your needs increase later. The four solar panels are 11¾-inches-by-47½-inches each, and so fit handily on one side of the platform.

After measuring and marking the plywood, I used a 2-inch hole saw in my electric drill to cut holes for wiring. After this, I painted the entire platform with two coats of exterior house paint. Be sure to really cover the edges of the plywood, and the holes. Plywood is extremely vulnerable to delamination by water, so paint it well.

Install your panels by laying them flat on the plywood, starting at the bottom. Bend the electrodes so they project through the holes you've drilled. I blocked up the panels ½-inch from the bottom 2-by-4 lip. Silicone all the way around the panel, and set the next panel into position. Do this with all four.

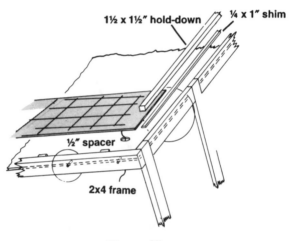

1½ x 1½" hold-down   ¼ x 1" shim

½" spacer

2x4 frame

Figure 17
Solar panel installation.

I put a ¼-inch ripping on each end, the thickness of a panel, and then installed a 1½-inch-by-1½-inch piece on each end to hold the panels down. Don't tighten the screws down too hard, you don't want to break the glass. Silicone around the 2-by-2, and the touch up paint.

For wiring, cut up an old extension cord, the thicker the better.

You want to connect these panels in *series*, not parallel (see Figure 18.) You'll hook up the positive of one panel to the negative of another, tying all four panels together, and ending up with one positive and one negative coming out of each end. These are your main power wires.

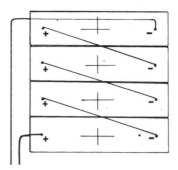

Figure 18
The panels should be wired in parallel: Hook the positive of one to the negative of the one next to it.

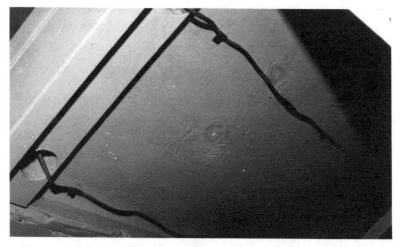

Figure 19
The underside wiring of a solar panel.

Note: If you install more than one complete set (four) of panels, you will need to wire the *sets* in *parallel*. Be clear on this. Each set of four panels is wired in series — negative to positive — with a final negative and positive wire coming out of each set. Then, to connect the sets together, wire the final negatives together, and the final positives together. This keeps the voltage the same (not to exceed 24 volts), but doubles the amperage output.

There are single panels on the market that put out the same voltage as a complete set (about 24 volts). If you use a single one of these, there are only two wires coming out, and they are your main power wires. Remember, these act as a complete set, and if you hook several of these together, you will need to wire them in *parallel*.

Regardless of the kind or number of panels you use, there is one thing you *must do* for all. You *must* ground the panels to earth. This is very important, because static electricity — which occurs with the approach of thunderstorms — can completely destroy your panels if they are not grounded.

Ground and earth mean the same thing — the ground underneath you. Don't ground to your trailer, this is not sufficient. Pound a $5 ground rod or a 5- or 6-foot piece of concrete reinforcing bar (rebar) into the ground next to your trailer, and attach a fairly heavy wire from the main negative wire of your panels to it. This is in addition to, and separate from, your main negative power wire running into your trailer. Hook your ground wire right there at the main negative coming out of your panels.

When wiring from your panels to the regulator, use a positive from one end of the set of panels, and the negative from the other end (the one that is tied into the ground wire). Mount the regulator in a convenient location according to its instructions (I mounted mine inside the trailer where I could see it) and run the wiring to it wherever it is convenient, keeping in mind that the shorter and thicker the wire is, the more voltage you get. From the regulator, run the wiring direct to the battery compartment.

I put my batteries in the storage area off the back of my trailer. It's best to keep them fairly warm, and this does it for me. Besides, that's where the wiring for the trailer's 12-volt lighting connects.

Next, hook up your batteries to each other in *parallel*. That is, positive to positive; negative to negative. This provides 12 volts with more amperage. You can use automotive battery cables from a department store, which I used initially, or simply make metal straps, as I did later.

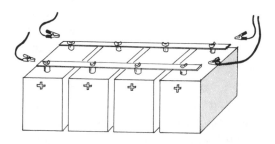

Figure 20
RV/Marine deep-cycle batteries should be hooked up in parallel.

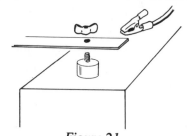

Figure 21
The first battery's connections.

Travel-Trailer Homesteading Under $5,000

Then, make the connection from the regulator wiring to the batteries, positive to positive; negative to negative. You can use small jumper cable-type ends for this, or crimp-on electrical connections you bolt to the battery terminals. You only need to connect to one battery or strap, because they are all tied together. Also connect the wires for your trailer's 12-volt lights somewhere on the batteries or straps.

From the batteries, run a line back into the trailer, wherever you want your main power to be. Again, the shorter and thicker the wire, the more voltage you get. At this location, install several cigarette-lighter sockets from an automobile. (I use the second outlet for my cellular phone.) On the back of the plugs, you'll see that the positive goes to the center of the inner socket, the negative to the outside screw-on casing. You now have a 12-volt power source in your trailer.

Get a voltmeter and install it somewhere easily seen from inside the trailer. The back wall is a good place. This meter allows you to monitor the charging and condition of your batteries. Install it "off-line." That is, don't run the plug or panel wiring through it; as you'll smoke it instantly. Instead, just run a couple of little wires directly to the batteries. I bought my voltmeter at Radio Shack for $5, but you can also take one out of an automobile dash if it's marked with numbers.

For 110 volts AC, you need a power inverter. These are available from many sources, including truck stops, and they are getting cheaper and more powerful all the time. I bought mine from the J.C. Whitney catalog. Figure up the biggest electrical load you need to run, and buy one of the appropriate size. I got the smallest "modified sine wave" inverter they had, a Statpower PROwatt 125, part number 83XX0598T. It cost $79.95, and puts out 125 watts continuously, 200 watts for five minutes, and a 400 watt surge. It runs my 13-inch color TV or word processor, no problem. Nowadays, you can get a 300-watt continuous unit for around $40. But regardless of

56

what kind you get, simply plug it into one of the cigarette lighter outlets you installed.

Presto — you have power!

A few notes:

Keep the solar panels clean for optimum performance. If you don't think this matters, go inside and watch the voltmeter while someone waves his hands over the panels.

Monitor your batteries via the voltmeter, even though they'll never overcharge if you use a regulator. By doing this, you'll understand and get used to your electrical usage, the charging trends, and the panel output in various weather conditions.

If your batteries are serviceable, check the water level every few months, and keep it up where it's supposed to be. Small bits of junk float up to the top of the water level, and if that level is down on the plates somewhere, the crud builds up between the plates and shorts them out. This is the reason many batteries fail in the first place.

Every once in a while, say, at three- to four-month intervals, you should set the switch on the regulator to "Equalize," and charge the hell out of the batteries. With the switch in this position, the regulator doesn't regulate at all, and with full sun you get a long, direct overcharge. This helps to keep crud from building up on the lead plates, and will extend the life of your batteries. The batteries should gas and/or boil for a while, but don't overdo it. Until you're used to doing this, start small, like a half-hour's worth. Next time, an hour, and build up from there. After a few times, you'll know when to quit. When you're finished with the equalization charge, put the switch back into the normal position and forget about it.

Don't drain your batteries down too far. Your inverter will cut out when the voltage drops to 10.7 volts, anyway, but I've never had this happen. In a charged battery, the water/electrolyte solution remains like sulfuric acid, and will not freeze. In a very weak battery, the solution becomes more like water. In cold weather a drained battery will freeze at about the same temperature as water.

This doesn't mean you can't use your power at night — quite to the contrary. That's what it's there for. Just don't drain your batteries down to nothing. If you use so much that the inverter shuts itself off, don't use the lights much beyond that.

If, for example, you use an excessive amount of power on a cloudy day, it's best to take a break the next day, and let the batteries get topped-off. It won't take long. How will you know when they are fully charged? The regulator shuts off the charging from the solar panels.

On cloudy days, your solar panels won't put out their maximum power. At times like this, if you need to, run the generator to charge the batteries. You simply run a cord from the 12-volt outlet on the generator to the battery straps, positive to positive, negative to negative.

An interesting alternative to solar panels (but one that didn't appeal to me), was done by a man near Blanca, Colorado. He bought a wrecked compact car — one that had been hit in the side and still had a good engine — and put it behind his trailer. He hung three more alternators on it and wired the output to his impressive collection of batteries. When the voltage got low enough, he went out and ran the car for an hour and charged his batteries up nicely.

One time, I also saw an alternator mounted on a pole, with some kind of fan blade on the front — a homemade wind generator. I don't know how well it worked, but I have my suspicions. Most wind generators I've seen are sitting idle, and not because of lack of wind — we get plenty of that. It's because they wear out quickly. Wind generators were a good idea when that's all they had, but with the advent of cheap, economical generators, and *especially* solar power, they were made obsolete.

An alternator turned by some kind of engine might be okay, but you'd still need some kind of voltage regulator, especially with 40 or 50 amps coming out of it. I don't care for the idea.

A New Life

I have heard that batteries can supposedly be reconditioned for a short time (if they're not too bad) by dumping the contents out, refilling the cells with distilled water, shaking the battery to dislodge the crud, dumping again, putting new electrolyte in, and then recharging. Whether that's true or not, I can't tell you. Maybe it works; maybe it's a vicious rumor.

At any rate, if you care for your batteries, you can expect four or five years of good service out of them. And should one ever fail, you can simply replace the bad one.

More power to ya....

Chapter Seven
Heat

Better figure on wood. Wood is the cheapest, most readily available way to heat a travel trailer or small mobile home.

Installing a wood stove in a travel trailer is not that hard to do — it takes about two days — and is the only way to heat and live cheaply at the same time. You'll back up your heat with propane, using the trailer's heater, but propane is expensive, and although you'll use some anyhow, you want to keep that to a minimum.

Stoves

My travel trailer is 8-feet-by-21-feet, and my stove, which is the shape of a small barrel laid on end, is substantially larger than I need. It is 16 inches in diameter, and 22 inches in depth, excluding the handle. I paid $80 for it at a used furniture store.

Try to get one that is as airtight as possible. They're more efficient, meaning they leak less, and use less wood. However, don't worry too much if it's not — it doesn't take much of a fire to heat the small space we have.

You don't need to spend a lot of money on the wood stove. Don't buy a fancy, brand name, super-expensive model. And it doesn't need to be lined with firebrick — a coal burner — unless it's a thin-walled model that's made that way. You won't burn coal, anyhow, unless you live next to a coal mine. Get one used, and don't be too concerned about looks. If you want to cook on it, get one that's set up for that.

Figure 22
The wood stove installed — good old country
comforts in the homestead.

Consider the best place to put it. In my case, I removed half of a built-in couch to put it in. It's between the couch and the kitchen sink, right next to the hot water heater.

Consider how you're going to vent it. What's the best way? Do you want to go through the roof? Or through a window? The wall?

In my case, I took out a window and replaced it with two sheets of sheet metal, one inside and one out. I had a sheet metal shop cut this for me, but you can certainly do it yourself. I simply measured the opening and had the metal cut to fit inside the aluminum jamb, against the stops. I also had the shop cut the holes for the stove pipe in it, making them just larger than the 6-inch flue.

On the floor I laid 2-inch solid cinder block, available at the lumberyard. At the back wall and the sides, I used 4-inch solid block, simply stacked up on top of each other, four courses high. If you want to get fancy, you can mortar the block, but I didn't.

Since my window is to the right of where the stove sits, I put a 45-degree elbow out the top of the stove, to direct the smoke towards the window. Next, I put a straight section with a damper in it, followed by a 90-degree elbow pointing at the window.

A straight section goes through the sheet metal, with small escutcheon (trim) plates on either side. Make it long enough to keep your flue 8 inches or so from the side of the trailer. Once outside, another 90-degree elbow turns upward, and three straight sections go up to a cap on top.

Figure 23
The wood stove flue should go through the middle of the window space, away from combustible areas.

Put the hole for the flue in the middle of the window space. This area will get hot, and you don't want the flue too close to anything combustible.

Consider whether you want your pipes to slip over or into each other. Slipping over each other is the way it is usually done, and I did this when I first installed my stove. In other words, the upper pipe slips down over the lower pipe. However, this allows condensation and creosote to flow freely from the joints, making a mess all over the outside of your trailer, and sometimes inside.

Some people reverse the pipes, as I have done. This makes any liquids flow all the way back down into the stove, not staining the side of your trailer. This is the way it is done in Europe. If you do this, make sure your 45-degree elbow out of your stove is a solid piece, not adjustable. Adjustable elbows leak stinky liquids all over your stove, and generally make a mess. If you can't find a solid one, seal the joints somehow. Another possibility is to install a piece of aluminum inside the joint where the elbow meets the straight piece. Make it long enough so the liquids drip into the stove (see Figure 24). Don't use a regular piece of metal, such as from skirting. I tried this, and it rusted out.

The flue must extend up beyond the top of your trailer. Tall flues work better, and you don't want any sparks falling onto your roof.

An installation like this is generally self-supporting, but you will need to strap the flue to the trailer because of wind. Use wire, metal strapping, or whatever's handy, but tie it down.

Clean the flue frequently. I do mine every three months, whether it needs it or not. Take it off in sections and run a stick through it.

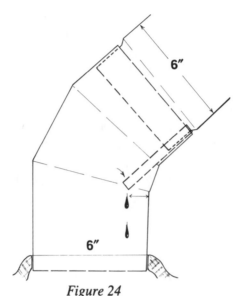

Figure 24
*A drip trough allows liquids and creosote to drip back
into the stove — not down the outside of the stovepipe.*

The Propane Heater

All travel trailers of this size have them. The older ones, like mine, amount to a space heater enclosed in a grill. Mine has a Coleman wall heater built in near the door, with a thermostat near the center of the trailer. Newer ones are required by law to be forced-air, meaning it has a blower attached. If yours does, you'll have to power the blower with your batteries. I prefer the old kind. But whatever kind you have, the unit must be functional.

Frequently, older heaters like this leak fumes. Mine did, too. But you can fix this with a product called "Furnace Cement," available in a hardware store. It comes in small tubs the size of a coffee cup, and costs about $2. There are two kinds: gray and black. The gray is more like mortar, and the black is more gooey. I prefer the black; it's easier to use, and holds better. Go over the seams generously, and also where the vent comes out. Let this cement dry for a day, and you should be in good shape.

Consider getting a propane tank from your local gas company. Changing little bottles all the time gets to be a chore. In winter, I found I had to fill one every four days, so I rented a 250-gallon tank from our local co-op. It costs $4 a month.

The total cost for delivery, gas line to the trailer, hookup, and 100 gallons of fuel was $241.

Wood

Heating with wood is simply the best way to go if you cut it yourself, or at least can get it cheap.

Out here, there are various ways to get your wood supply. Most Bureau of Land Management and Forest Service areas will issue you permits to cut your own. Some are free, but you have to drive a ways to get there, so the gas burned is a factor. Other permits cost $10 a cord. (A cord, incidentally, is a loosely stacked pile of wood that is 4 feet tall, 4 feet deep, and 8 feet long.)

A few large mountain ranches offer a "woodfest" every year, sometimes twice, where you can go and cut aspen for $5 a truckload. Occasionally, someone will let you cut for free on their land, to clear out the dead stuff.

There is also slab wood, which you can get from the sawmill for $20 a bundle. Slab wood comes from the outside cuttings of pine logs that the mill has sawed into lumber, and a bundle is about three-quarters of a cord. Sure, there are a few toothpicks in it, and a little bark here and there, but most is good stuff, with a few good, thick chunks thrown in. Sometimes, you'll find dimensional lumber in it, pieces you can use around the homestead. And there are other uses for slabs, too. Some people use it for siding on porches or sheds. The way some of these curious-looking pieces come, you could make pioneer-style furniture, if you've a mind to.

The mill crew will load the bundle into your truck with a forklift, and the price is right, considering aspen goes for around $85 a cord, and piñon about $100 or more, depending on the time of year. Naturally, most wood costs more to buy in the fall and winter, when demand is high. Slab wood costs $20 all year around.

Slab wood is usually dry when you get it, and only a handful of pieces need to be split. But even if it's green, it ages fast, and you can start burning the green stuff in about a week. You'll still need to cut it for length, and this is best done while it's still in your truck, bundled and banded. Just start at one end, and cut as deep as your saw will go — it's easy cutting, too. Move down the line making your incisions, then shut the saw off and clear off the cut pieces. Then repeat the process until you're down to within a few inches of the truck bed. You'll want to pull out those last few layers and cut them on the tailgate or a sawbuck.

I now use a combination of slabwood and piñon for my heat, along with whatever is left over in the woodpile. The pine slabs start easily, and make a good cool-weather fire. At night, or when it's really cold, I start with slabs, and then put in the heavy-duty stuff, the piñon. Bank a fire with piñon and it lasts a long, long time.

I cut my permit-piñon over on "the mountain," which is all of 4 miles from my homestead. Some people don't bother with permits, and take their chances on a ticket for trespassing, although I've never heard of any getting caught. Others buy a permit or two, and then cut all they want. Myself, I buy and use the permits honestly, although I've never seen a ranger up there.

Naturally, dry wood burns better than wet, and wood dries by being cut, split, stacked, and aged. You just have to do it. And if you're like me, you'll enjoy it.

Hard woods burn better than soft, that is, they last longer and burn hotter. However, soft woods are easier to cut and split, and generally season faster.

How to tell soft woods from hard: needles or leaves. Soft woods have needles — for example, pine, spruce, and fir. Hard woods have leaves — oak, maple, and such.

There are exceptions. Piñon, which has needles, is very hard — hard to cut and split, and long to dry. But it burns long and hot. Aspen, which has leaves, is soft. It's easy to split and dries quickly. But it also burns quickly.

A few words on chain saws: You get what you pay for. You can spend $500 on a Stihl that will last a decade or longer, or you can buy a new McCulloch Eager Beaver on sale for just over $100, and it will last for several years.

I go with the 14-inch Beaver. It's a very reliable saw, but wears out with really tough work. It's kind of like a disposable tool, but if you treat it well, keep it sharp, and don't cut firewood for a living, it should last you at least several years. I buy a new one every two or three years. Watch for them on sale every fall at department stores.

To sharpen a chain saw, get a round metal file of the appropriate size, wherever chain saws are sold. The smaller chains use a $5/32$-inch file, and it doesn't need a handle on it. For best results, *pull* the file through the tooth, don't push it. And you file only "one-way." File "out," and don't drag the file back over the tooth, it wears the file out, not to mention dulling the tooth you just sharpened. Don't worry about "letting down" the guide links in front of the teeth. By the time you need to do this, the chain will be shot anyhow.

A chain saw is a marvelous tool, and I certainly hope the person who invented it became a millionaire. But do be careful using one; read the instructions in the box. You needn't worry about what a chain will do if it breaks; it will simply sling out ahead of you into a neat little pile on the ground.

Splitting wood is great exercise. For the harder or thicker woods, use a sledgehammer and wedge, or a maul. The old double-headed axes work wonders on the soft stuff.

There's really not much to splitting wood. Do it when the wood has aged a little, and start at the center. For those of you who've never done it, you'll be surprised at how easily you'll pick it up, and how much satisfaction it gives you. I really enjoy it, and still split the softer woods by hand, even though a friend gave me his old hydraulic splitter.

I don't know what it is, but splitting wood is kind of like hunting. Maybe it brings out some kind of long-buried instinctive response in me. I just know it feels good to chop wood.

Fires

I use kerosene to start cold fires. Just throw a few pieces of wood in the stove and squirt a little kerosene on it. A plastic dish-soap or syrup bottle works well for this. Kerosene won't explode when you light it; instead it flares up slowly. It doesn't take much; you'll soon find out how much to use.

A word of caution: Light only *cold* fires with this. If there are any red coals at all, it's best to just stir up the fire and leave the door open until it catches. Kerosene squirted on red coals will start vaporizing, and will *foomp!* when lit.

Some people use diesel fuel, and it acts about the same way. I use kerosene because I have it on hand anyway for my kerosene lamp.

Incidentally, I don't use a grate in my wood stove. When you burn wood constantly, you have to empty the ashes weekly. The grate is just a pain in the neck at such times, and keeping logs on the coals is one way to keep them burning, especially if they're not completely dried yet. Just stir the fire up occasionally, and everything will burn completely.

You'll soon find that a fire uses up all the fresh air in a trailer. Just crack a window open. Sometimes, if it's really windy, you'll find that you may get smoke coming out of the stove. Open a window upstream, close the others, and that usually takes care of it. For this reason, I don't recommend putting plastic over the windows of the trailer. The wind can be very fickle, and on different days you'll have different windows open. I also don't recommend covering the vent in the top of the trailer. It's easy to build a fire that is too hot, and opening the vent is the quickest way to dump the hot air.

At night, or anytime you are leaving the trailer for hours at a time, turn down the stove by closing the air vents nearly all the way, and closing the flue damper most of the way. You'll notice that this immediately makes the wood stove hotter, but this is because the heat is no longer going out the flue, and is effectively bottled up in the stove. However, this is short lived, and the fire goes down because of lack of air to burn, because you have closed the air vents. Because of closing the damper, most of the smoke remains within the stove, and smoke doesn't contain much oxygen.

Chapter Eight
Refrigeration

Figure 25
A travel-trailer kitchen has all the comforts.

A trailer of this size generally has a small propane refrigerator installed in it as factory equipment. Many, however, no longer work. That is usually not a problem.

The propane refrigerator in mine had been removed and replaced with an apartment-sized, electric unit. Naturally, my small generator wouldn't power that, and in any case, it wouldn't work because I would have had to run the generator around the clock. A generator that never stops, will, sooner or later, wear out.

When I first came out here, I installed an icebox. It was fall, and as the cold weather progressed, I was soon able to make my own ice by setting a tray of water outside overnight. This worked well, but still left no freezer capacity, with the exception of a cooler placed in the shade on the north side of my trailer. The cooler works plenty well in freezing temperatures, of course, but as soon as it started to warm up, the food spoiled.

Next, I tried using a good-sized 12-volt "Igloo" cooler. They're pretty good for a road trip in your car, but suck the living daylights out of your batteries at home. Your system simply cannot keep up with it. I tried; it just wouldn't work. I had to go back to propane.

After talking with my neighbor, who uses two full-sized propane refrigerators in his mobile home, I obtained a small propane unit from another trailer. The man had tried it, and it didn't work.

People commonly believe these to use a lot of fuel, but a propane refrigerator of this size actually required less money to operate in warm weather than the cost of buying block ice every other day, and gives you a small freezer in the bargain.

Aside from the coolant itself, there are no moving parts, and a propane refrigerator uses only a small pilot light for operation. The unit must be vented outside, of course, but trailers of this size are generally already set up for this.

These units operate on a liquid-to-gas and gas-back-to-liquid basis, the gas flame (heat) providing the means of transfer. The liquid refrigerant is turned into gas by the heat. It rises in the piping. As it rises, it cools. As it then cools back into a liquid, it produces a cold temperature, which directly cools the food compartment.

A refrigerator of this type *must* be level, as the piping is designed to work by gravity. Use your level on this, both directions.

As long as your unit is level, has refrigerant in it, and a flame, it should work. If it doesn't, what generally goes wrong with these boxes is one of two things: Either the refrigerant has leaked out, which is rare, or, more likely, the refrigerant settles from lack of use and doesn't perform adequately.

If it has leaked out, you might be able to have it recharged by an appliance repairperson, if you can find one who works on them. However, leakage is usually not the problem, and the next method of making them operable should be tried first.

Remove the unit from the trailer, completely. Blow all gas lines out, including the filter, if it has one (it looks like a small automotive gas line filter). Make sure there's no soot in the flue by taking the cover off and pulling out the squiggly little heat baffle. (You'll see what I mean.) Next, clean out the orifices in the gas burner with a small needle, pin, or something of that sort, being careful not to enlarge the holes (propane consumption would increase, and your refrigerator might over-perform, meaning you might not be able to keep the temperature high enough to keep the entire food compartment from freezing).

Then, put the unit upside-down in the back of your truck, and leave it there (with all gas lines or orifices taped over) for several days, and go about your business. If it gurgles when you turn it over, it has refrigerant in it. Just being turned on its head for several days is usually enough to stir up the refrigerant. This is called "burping" the unit. However, I drove around with it in the back of my truck for three days, as I conducted my day-to-day affairs, believing this would *really* help stir it up.

After several days, reinstall it, checking the gas line connections for leaks. Then light the flame, and give it twenty-four hours to cool enough for use. This usually does it. If it doesn't, try burping it again. If it still doesn't work, check the burner.

Possibly, the two-stage pilot light (burner) is malfunctioning for some reason. Check to be sure that it works in two stages by turning the temperature control from defrost to operation. The flame should rise when the knob is turned, but the rise is very small indeed, and you have to pay attention to catch it. These things don't use much gas.

By stirring up the contents thus, you should have a full functional refrigerator with freezer. These actually work very well, indeed.

Figure 26
A propane refrigerator this size costs less to run than
buying ice and has the added advantage of a freezer.

An interesting note: The area where I live is windy at times, and I found that a strong, sustained wind affected the operation of my refrigerator — it started defrosting because the wind was blowing the heat of the flame away. I closed one side of the vent on top of the trailer — the side facing the pre-vailing wind — and partially covered the air intake on the side of the trailer. That took care of the problem.

Chapter Nine
Mobile Homesteading

Figure 27
Travel-trailer living can be adapted for a mobile home.

All of the technology described in previous chapters can also be applied to a mobile home, and I have done this. Really, there's not much difference, except size. In fact, you could even set up a cabin or small house this way.

A mobile home also comes on wheels, only usually more of them. You still set it on blocks, and the skirting is the same. It uses the same septic system, and water still comes from a cistern. It's powered by solar, and heated by wood. Propane still heats water and cools food.

You have a lot more room, but it comes with a price.

I switched to a mobile home for a variety of reasons. My income rose, and I wanted to upgrade my lifestyle. My writing expanded, and I wanted a separate study. I also figured to make this my last home, and while I'm working, wanted to put in everything I wanted before I retired to writing.

The Installation and Skirting

Since the requirements for land are the same, I'll go right into the shelter itself.

If you can get a mobile home cheap, the costs of setting up a homestead are nearly the same. It can be done, but you don't just find these bargains everywhere.

My brother bought his mobile home for $800. Another guy I know paid $1400, then sold the furnace out of it to recoup some of his cost. I paid a lot more for mine, and kept the furnace (which I recommend).

You'll have to carefully consider the moving and setup. Does it have axles under it? Can you pull it with a pickup? Is a permit required to move it, and do you really need to get one? Are the tires in good shape?

If you can get the owner to throw in setup with the purchase, even better. Remember, everything is negotiable. Of course, you'll want to be there if you have them deliver it. Don't take it for granted they'll put it exactly where you told them to; you might come home and find it backwards.

Before you bring the trailer onto the property, be sure and clean off the spot where it will sit. Use a shovel or whatever you need. You'll be crawling around under there for setup and skirting, not to mention any improvements or repairs.

It's not necessary to pull the trailer tires up on boards. In fact, you may even want to dig some small holes for the tires, depending on how high the trailer sits. Give consideration to this, according to how you will skirt it.

Think about whether you want to tie your mobile home down. If you do, dig and pour concrete pits with a bent rebar in the top of them. An alternative is to buy tie-downs that screw into the ground.

If you set it up yourself, I'd recommend using concrete blocks. These are available at any lumberyard. The spacing depends on the size of the trailer. Eight feet is good, and I'd go no more than 10 feet apart.

You'll need a good-sized hydraulic bottle jack and a good level. And I do mean a good level. Don't use some old beat-up thing, or a cheap aluminum handyman special. Buy a good wood level, one that does not have adjustable vials. If you don't bang it around, adjustments are not necessary, as the vials are fixed in proper position. Don't drop it, and take good care of it.

Wood wedges will come in handy on top of the concrete blocks for smaller adjustments. Start with flat blocks on the ground, 2 or 3 inches thick, and put your concrete blocks on top of them, on edge. This means the two hollows in the blocks will go straight up, just like they're used for buildings. Don't put them any other way; this is the only way a block has any strength.

Use your level on the trailer frame, starting at one end. There will be two main beams under the trailer. Level across from one to the other, and put a block "pier" under each one. Because your level won't reach from one beam to the other, use a straight piece of lumber like a 2-by-4, and put your level against this, in the middle of the board.

Once you've got the end level, start moving down the run by placing the level on the underside of the beams, first one, then the other. Move on, from time to time checking across to the other beam with the level and 2-by-4. Make adjustments as necessary.

The mobile home is skirted in the same fashion as a travel-trailer, although it takes more material. If your home sits up higher you may want to turn the skirting on end. There is usually a metal lip at the bottom of the trailer's siding that the skirting slides under, and you can screw to this. You'll still need the 1- or 2-by-4s at the seams, and don't forget the access panels. I insulated my skirting with blue Styrofoam insulation because I got it for free. While you're under there, put some mouse poison in a few locations, just for good measure.

The Septic System

I'm using the existing system, and simply capped off the travel-trailer line and trenched a new one to my mobile home, observing the same ¼-inch-to-the-foot slant. I cut a new hole in the first barrel and siliconed it in. It was a smelly job, but that just assures me the system is working properly.

The mobile home uses standard 4-inch sewer line, and no adapter was needed to make the connection. I still put bacteria down the toilet regularly, and have no problems with the system.

Water

I installed a larger cistern in a new location nearer my mobile home. I bartered for a larger barrel, and piped it in basically the same way, except that the barrel is outside of the skirting, not under the trailer. Be sure to slope the PVC pipe that your pump line runs inside of back to the cistern. The same little cistern pump is used, and I put two barrels in the house where the washer and dryer hookups are. To support the weight, the barrels rest on a piece of 1-inch plywood laid over the floor, which in turn is over one of the beams that rests on a block pier.

Between the barrels I ran a siphon hose, so that the water level in both remains the same. From out of the top of one of the barrels, I ran ½-inch PVC up to an RV water pump. From the pump, wired to the batteries above, I ran a connector hose (which I got from the hardware store) and hooked it up to the washer cold water line, and this pressurizes the entire house.

I use the existing hot water heater, and have hot and cold running water at the turning of a faucet. I no longer take a Navy shower, either, making a long, hot shower one of my few luxuries. However, I did install a water-saving shower head.

I did allow my water usage to rise, and bought a water-hauling tank for my truck. I had thoughts about draining the roof into the cistern during the so-called rainy season, but have since met a man with a drilling rig. The well will be installed next spring. Of course, this will necessitate a bigger generator to power the well pump.

Power

Power is the same: solar backed up by generator.

I built a new platform for my solar panels and attached it to the south side of the mobile home. I also installed a heavy-duty platform above the water barrels in the house, where the batteries sit. This is my power center, where the regulator and inverter are mounted. I also mounted the switches for the pressure pump, cistern, and solar panels here. The side wall holds my voltmeter and telephone.

Figure 28
Solar panels backed up by a bulldozer battery and a
generator provide enough electricity for a larger space.

Speaking of telephones, I now have a new wireless phone service that uses my cell phone. There are no air-time charges, and it costs and works the same as a regular phone. It requires an $85 antenna and a $5 reprogramming of the phone. They tell me you can even get the Internet on it, although it will be somewhat slow. Look for the service coming soon to a location near you.

From the inverter, I ran Romex electrical wire under the house to the various rooms for lights and other things. I simply put a plug end on the line at the inverter, and another in the rooms, where I use fluorescent lights.

Yes, I use more power, but with the addition of a second set of panels and a bulldozer battery, it's no problem.

I still use the same little generator for battery charging on cloudy days. It sits out back, and the wires run through the wall to the batteries, although I hardly use it.

Heat

Heat is also the same: a wood stove backed up by propane.

Figure 29
A mobile home allows enough space to run
the pipe straight through the roof.

There are some special considerations to think of. For one, if your mobile home will be insured, you'll need to check with the insurance company. Some companies prohibit wood stoves. Others have special distance-from-combustibles requirements. Most will insist on photographs of the installation.

In a mobile home, you have much more room for the wood stove, so do it right. Don't just carve a hole in the wall or go through the window. Buy a regular chimney kit and go straight up through the roof. Directions are included with the materials, and make sure you do it correctly — improper wood stove installations are the leading cause of fires in mobile homes.

Get the best wood stove you can afford. The better the stove, the less wood you'll use, and you'll get more heat. Somebody gave me an old Ashley brand, and it works great. However, I use nearly three times more wood than I did in the travel-trailer. Do I mind? No.

Incidentally, if you have a wood stove with broken or missing firebrick in it, not to worry. You can get new firebrick at the lumberyard for about $1.25 each. Installation is quite easy. Unbolt the retaining iron, clean out all remaining pieces, put the new brick into place, and re-bolt the retainers. It must be real firebrick, as all others will disintegrate from the heat.

You'll need to trench in a new gas line from your propane tank and connect the trailer, but this is easily done, and seldom requires more than one adapter fitting. Be sure to check out your new connections for leaks — and all lines in the mobile home — by using a spray bottle mixture of soapy water on all Ts, unions, and connections. Be safe, not sorry.

For back-up heat, I installed a propane space heater in the hallway by the bathroom. This is good for when you are away, and also so you don't have to get up in the middle of the night to stoke the wood stove. Again, check with your insurance company and install it right.

Before I insulated my skirting, I found the need to run the furnace to unfreeze water pipes on minus 10° mornings. This was easily accomplished by running Romex from the furnace to the outside, where I plugged it into the generator. The little Honda will run the blower, but it's a chore. Additionally, I yanked out the floor ducts and covered over the vents, so the heat would flow between the floor and the trailer's bottom insulation (not the skirting) where the water pipes run.

Refrigeration

There's still only one way to go: propane. But you can choose between a camper type or a full-sized unit. I have used both in my mobile home, and prefer the larger. These are even harder to come by, and cost considerably more.

You can buy a new one from a propane dealer for about $1,300, or use a small one like I did until a used one comes along. I got an old Servel for $200, and had to spend a whole day cleaning the soot out of the burner and getting it into shape, but am very pleased with the results. One homesteader I know placed a "wanted" ad in his local paper. A man replied after several days, saying to come and take *two* refrigerators, free for the hauling. And they both work.

Chances are, you'll have to T into your propane stove line and run ¼-inch copper gas line to the refrigerator. This is easily bendable, to keep hidden away in cabinets. Measure up the distance, and have the lumberyard cut it, flare the ends, and give you the appropriate fittings. Put a valve somewhere in this line so you can leave everything else lit if you need to burp the refrigerator at some later date.

As I said, mobile homesteading comes with a price, and I was willing to pay it. But naturally, like any person, I sometimes doubt my decision. I really enjoy the extra room — especially a full-sized study to write in — and having a regular "home." But my taxes went up some, I put more time and money into maintenance, and cleaning the house takes much longer. It also takes three times the wood to heat, and uses more propane and water.

Like I said, it was worth it to me, but I sometimes reminisce about living in the travel-trailer, and the good times I had in it.

Figure 30
Mobile homesteading has tradeoffs for more room:
higher taxes, more maintenance and more resources
such as wood and water. But it's worth it.

Here are some of the projects I have planned for the future:

- Outside air for the woodstove. I'll run about a 4-inch duct from the outside to the air intake on my woodstove. This way, I won't have to leave a window open.

- The well, which shouldn't cost me more than about $500.

- A washing machine. I'll install a water dispersion pit outside, instead of running the used water through the septic.

- A hot tub (see the next chapter). Can you imagine that? A homesteading friend made one, and has given me a solar hot water panel for this.

- A garage and a pole barn.

- And finally, *very* early retirement. I have several other books started that I want to finish.

Chapter Ten
The Hot Tub According to Bob

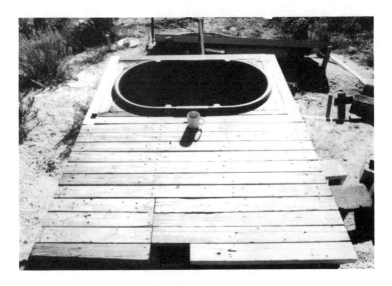

Figure 31
The homesteader's reward.

Oftentimes I've visited friends in the city who had a hot tub, and considered not having one to be the only drawback to homesteading. I'd wracked my brains trying to figure out how to build one, but still kept coming up against the inevitable:

Travel-Trailer Homesteading Under $5,000

How to heat and move the water without having a big, noisy generator running all the time. There didn't seem to be a solution, but guess what?

A fellow homesteader and friend by the name of Bob Herman came up with a great idea for a hot tub, and here's what makes it work: a tub, solar water-heating panel, some pipe, and water. Sounds pretty simple, huh? It is, and I can't believe I didn't think of it myself.

Figure 32
Bob's hot tub. Notice the insulated
hot water line from panel.

Because Bob also hauls his water, he wanted something that didn't use too much of that precious liquid. This fit the bill perfectly.

He bought a 100-gallon poly-stock tank to use as a tub for $70, picked up an old solar collector, and used wood and pipe from his junk pile. (See? I told you it pays to save most everything.)

Starting with a platform, he enclosed the tub with old 2-by-4s. Then he set his water-heating panel in place, lower than the tub and facing south.

Figure 33
Imagine a sunset soak...
How do you spell relief?

From the collector (or heater) he ran the hot line to the tub, placing it near the top, but still under the water level. The cold water line comes out of the tub near the bottom, and returns to the heating panel.

This system works by itself, on the principle of thermosiphoning. Water heated by the sun rises out of the heating panel and flows into the tub. And because hot water rises, it naturally follows that cooler water sinks. So when the cool water settles to the bottom, it is siphoned off into the return line. From there it is pulled back to the collector, to be reheated and start the process all over again.

Because Bob won't use chemicals, he changes his water about once a week via a drain valve. This is not a problem, however, because he lives so close to his water source, and the used water goes directly onto his garden.

Build yourself a hot tub, fill it with water, put a lid on it to retain the heat, and let the sun do its work.

Figure 34
The hot tub with insulated lid in place.

What could be any simpler than this? I don't know why I didn't come up with it first, but I'll tell you this: I'll be building mine first chance I get. And that doesn't leave any drawbacks to travel-trailer homesteading, does it?

Chapter Eleven
What It's Like to Live This Way

I have been homesteading for five years now, and believe me when I tell you that without a doubt, these have been the best years of my life. Do I have any regrets? Yes, that I didn't do this sooner!

This is clean living at its finest. It's quiet, and there is time to think. There is peace.

If you decide to homestead, you'll lead a fit and active lifestyle. (We call it hard work.) You'll grow stronger, thinner, and wiser. Your trousers will mysteriously get bigger in the waist, and you'll hook into those never-used buckle holes *waaaaay* up there on your belt.

You'll breathe the cleanest air, and your endurance will improve. You'll be tanned, confident, and self-reliant.

One day, you'll be out working on the spread, and you'll know why you're smiling. You'll stop, look around, and wonder — as I did — why you didn't do this sooner.

What you are going to do is surprise yourself!

Indeed, this will be a learning experience. You'll learn a million things, like:

Travel-Trailer Homesteading Under $5,000

How many stars there really are, and the names of some of the constellations.

There really can be shadows from starlight.

"Shooting stars" doesn't mean murdering Hollywood celebrities, and that they sometimes split in two.

Just how many satellites there are, and their main orbits.

There are still millions of animals living in the wild, and you don't have to go to the zoo to see them.

Why a pair of binoculars is a necessity.

How it is that the people around you will know who you are before you meet them.

A gun, besides being a weapon, is also a tool.

A bullet will not go as far as you think.

A round shot straight up will not kill you when it comes down (it won't drop any faster than a rock).

Four-wheel-drives are addictive (once you own one, you'll never be without one again).

Four-wheel-drive is often more important than gas mileage.

Local dialects have a way of creeping into your speech.

There is no "Z" in the word diesel.

Country people are not dumb.

Antlers will dress up nearly any wall. They're not called "horns." That's the thing that doesn't work in your truck.

Why late-season hunting is the best. (Hey, I'm not gonna tell you everything.)

UPS actually *does* deliver world-wide.

Pizza Hut does not.

Silence is not deafening at all.

Traffic jams are not compulsory, but door jambs are.

East is least, and West is best. (Sorry, couldn't help that.)

A Western sunset is worth a thousand pictures.

Some mothers *still do* name their boys Royce, Cleatus, and Wes.

"Ma'am" is still a respectable way to address women.

Women like to hear, "Yes, Ma'am." Girls do not.

Cameras don't work well in sub-zero temperatures.

Pac boots do.

When your nostrils freeze together, your camera doesn't work, and the snow squeaks under your pac boots, it's below zero.

Humidity and lack of sunshine had a lot to do with how cold you were before.

Some others are:

Deals can still be done on a handshake.

A man's word is more important than money.

Being free is more important than money.

There are *lots* of things more important than money.

Spring cleaning is really not necessary.

It pays to save most everything.

Rifle racks complement any pickup truck.

Figure 35
A tractor will head up your wish list.

Automobiles last twice as long when the salt goes on your meat instead of your street.

Travel-Trailer Homesteading Under $5,000

The correct name for the man who shoes your horses is blacksmith, not "fairy-er."

Why a tractor will head up your wish list.

Need outweighs want.

Why people keep that black teapot on the woodstove.

A day spent working on your homestead is much longer than a day spent working in a factory.

The exact same beverage tastes three times better when you drink it in your new homestead.

You sunburn faster in thinner air.

Your truck needs an electric fuel pump in thinner air.

"Fired" has nothing to do with your job, but everything to do with your rifle.

What the difference is between a buck and a bull.

Antelope are fast, curious animals that taste bad.

"Ky-yotes" (not ky-yo-tees) are ugly critters that make a beautiful sound.

Your dog does not care for ky-yotes in the least.

The rattles of a dead rattlesnake make for exciting entertainment when shaken near unsuspecting city folk around the campfire.

Cowboy hats serve many useful purposes.

"That's a lie!" does not refer to where your golf ball sits on the green.

A "bastard" is a file that you will need.

The Frenchy words *cul de sac* do not translate into Western English.

Neither do "animal rights."

Trees grow back.

Tree-hugging is acceptable behavior only during hurricanes and tornadoes.

Hurricanes and tornadoes are extremely rare in the mountains.

It's difficult to heat your house with spotted owls.

You can tell when your stovepipe needs cleaning by the smell.

"Busted" means broke, not arrested.

People will take you at your word, unless you show them otherwise.

If you show them otherwise, they will never forget it.

The Western word for hair stylist is "barber."

Barbers are cheaper than hair stylists.

The grocery store gives you free dry ice in the summer.

Dry ice is what keeps your groceries cold, it is not a rap musician.

Rap is not music, and Bob Dole was right.

On the lighter side, you may also learn these few goodies:

"Pot" is a roast, not something you smoke.

"Grass" is a weed that grows in your yard.

"Weeds" are to be burned, not smoked.

"Reefer" is a refrigeration unit for your semi.

"Reefer madness" is when that unit breaks down.

"Red-eyed" is what you are after you illegally drove your semi all night long to get home.

A "number" is what you use to get your neighbor on the line.

A "bong" is the sound when those servants hit that giant gong with a big hammer in those Egyptian movies, not something you smoke something with.

A "doobie" is one of those funny-looking German dogs.

"Wow!" is the second half of your funny-looking dog's two-word vocabulary, not something you say after you smoke something.

"Right on" is part of the directions to Billy-Bob's farm.

"Far out" is where you live, not what you say after you smoke something.

"Out of sight" is how far in the hole you used to be.

Travel-Trailer Homesteading Under $5,000

"Munchies" are those funny little guys in *The Wizard of Oz*, aren't they?

Out here, a "flower child" carries the flowers down the aisle at somebody's wedding.

A "buzz" is something the barber gives you.

"Cool!" is what it's going to be like when you get up at three in the morning to stoke the wood stove.

And "crash" is what happens when the brakes fail on your pickup, not what you do after you smoke something.

But seriously, you'll also learn about God's Country, and the mountains sometimes *do* touch the sky.

And, that you can be much freer than you *ever* thought possible. Really!

Chapter Twelve
Closing Statement

I sincerely hope you enjoyed this book, and are full of ideas about how to prepare for a new life homesteading.

If you don't already have a truck, you should get one, preferably a four-wheel drive. Gather all your tools beforehand — look for bargains and visit garage sales for things you'll need.

Try to get all your bills paid off, and stash something away you can live on while you're setting up your homestead. If you have money, you can concentrate on getting your home set up, without the additional pressure of looking for a job — or giving all your time to it — and then trying to work around your home in your spare time. In my case, it took me a little while, but I saved until I had a year's worth of expenses in the bank. Let me tell you, it's a wonderful feeling to be set up on your own property, and not owe anybody *anything*.

You'll know it's worth it when there's an eagle on your fence-post, antelope in your yard, or a bear at your mailbox; when your dog runs free (and so do you), the bills are gone, and the pressure's off. Take a moment to imagine that.

Hey, life is short, and roses don't last forever.

The best of luck to you, my friend.

Other Titles of Interest:

HOW TO BUY LAND CHEAP
Fifth Edition
by Edward Preston

This is the bible of bargain-basement land buying. The author bought eight lots for a total sum of $25. He shows you how to buy good land all over the country for not much more. This book has been revised, with updated addresses and new addresses added. This book will take you through the process for finding cheap land, evaluating and bidding on it, and closing the deal. Sample form letters are also included to help you get started and get results. You can buy land for less than the cost of a night out — this book shows how. *1996, 5½ x 8½, 136 pp, illustrated, soft cover.* $14.95.

SELF-SUFFICIENCY GARDENING
Financial, Physical and Emotional Security
From Your Own Backyard
by Martin P. Waterman

A practical guide to organic gardening techniques that will enable anyone to grow vegetables, fruits, nuts, herbs, medicines and other useful products, thereby increasing self-sufficiency and enhancing the quality of life. Includes sections on edible landscaping; greenhouses; hydroponics and computer gardening (including the Internet); seed saving and propagation; preserving and storing crops; and much more, including fact-filled appendices. The author is a highly regarded journalist and gardener, world-recognized fruit breeder and is a director of the North American Fruit Explorers. *1995, 8½ x 11, 128 pp, illustrated, indexed, soft cover.* $13.95.

SHELTERS, SHACKS AND SHANTIES
by D.C. Beard

A fascinating book with more than 300 pen-and-ink illustrations and step-by-step instructions for building various types of shelters. The emphasis is on simplicity with easy-to-use tools such as hatchets and axes. Fallen tree shelters • Indian wicki-ups • sod houses • elevated shacks and shanties • tree houses • caches • railroad tie shacks • pole houses • log cabins • and many more. One of the great classics of outdoor lore. *1914, 5 x 7, 259 pp, illustrated, soft cover.* $9.95.

HOW TO LIVE WITHOUT ELECTRICITY
— AND LIKE IT
by Anita Evangelista

There's no need to remain dependent on commercial electrical systems for your home's comforts and security. This book describes many alternative methods that can help you become more self-reliant and free from the utility companies. Learn how to light, heat and cool your home, obtain and store water, cook and refrigerate food, and fulfill many other household needs without paying the power company! This book contains photographs, illustrations, and mail-order listings to make your transition to independence a snap! *1997, 5½ x 8½, 168 pp, illustrated, soft cover.* $13.95.

FREEDOM ROAD
by Harold Hough

Have you dreamed about leaving the rat race but don't know where to start? This book will show you how to make a plan, eliminate your debts, and buy an RV. You'll learn about beautiful places where you can live for free. You'll learn how to make all the money you'll need from your hobbies. And you'll learn how to live a comfortable, healthy lifestyle on just a few dollars a day. Do the things you've been putting off: spending time with family, getting healthy, and being free! Why wait for retirement when you can live a low-cost, high travel lifestyle today! *1991, 5½ x 8½, 174 pp, illustrated, soft cover.* $16.95.

BACKYARD MEAT PRODUCTION
by Anita Evangelista

If you're tired of paying ever-soaring meat prices, and worried about unhealthy food additives and shoddy butchering techniques, then you should start raising small meat-producing animals at home! You needn't live in the country, as most urban areas allow for this practice. This book clearly explains how to raise rabbits, chickens, quail, pheasants, guineas, ducks, and mini-goats and -pigs for their meat and by-products, which can not only be consumed but can also be sold or bartered to specialized markets. Improve your diet while saving money and becoming more self-sufficient! *1997, 5½ x 8½, 136 pp, illustrated, soft cover.* $14.95.

COMMUNITY TECHNOLOGY
by Karl Hess
with an Introduction by Carol Moore

In the 1970s, the late Karl Hess participated in a five-year social experiment in Washington D.C.'s Adams-Morgan neighborhood. Hess and several thousand others labored to make their neighborhood as self-sufficient as possible, turning to such innovative techniques as raising fish in basements, growing crops on rooftops and in vacant lots, installing self-contained bacteriological toilets, and planning a methanol plant to convert garbage to fuel. There was a newsletter and weekly community meetings, giving Hess and others a taste of participatory government that changed their lives forever. *1979, 5½ x 8½, 120 pp, soft cover.* $9.95

HOW TO DEVELOP A LOW-COST
FAMILY FOOD-STORAGE SYSTEM
by Anita Evangelista

If you're weary of spending a large percentage of your income on your family's food needs, then you should follow this amazing book's numerous tips on food-storage techniques. Slash your food bill by over fifty percent, and increase your self-sufficiency at the same time through alternative ways of obtaining, processing and storing foodstuffs. Includes methods of freezing, canning, smoking, jerking, salting, pickling, krauting, drying, brandying and many other food-preservation procedures. *1995, 5½ x 8½, 120 pp, illustrated, indexed, soft cover.* $10.00.

THE WILD AND FREE COOKBOOK
With a Special Roadkill Section
by Tom Squier

Why pay top dollar for grocery-store food, when you can dine at no cost by foraging and hunting? Wild game, free of the steroids and additives found in commercial meat, is better for you, and many weeds and wild plants are more nutritious than the domestic fruits and vegetables found in the supermarket. Authored by a former Special Forces survival school instructor, this cookbook is chock full of easy-to-read recipes that will enable you to turn wild and free food (including roadkill!) into gourmet meals. *1996, 7¼ x 11½, 306 pp, illustrated, indexed, soft cover. $19.95.*

EAT WELL FOR 99¢ A MEAL
by Bill and Ruth Kaysing

Want more energy, more robust, vigorous health? Then you must eat food that can impart these well-being characteristics and this book will be your faithful guide. As an important bonus, you will learn how to save lots of money and learn how to enjoy three homemade meals a day for a cost of less than one dollar per meal. The book will tell you how to shop, how to stock your pantry, where to pick fresh foods for free, how to cook your 99¢ meal, what foods you can grow yourself, how to preserve your perishables, several recipes to get you started, and much much more. *1996, 5½ x 8½, 204 pp, illustrated, indexed, soft cover.* $14.95.

THE 99¢ A MEAL COOKBOOK
by Ruth and Bill Kaysing

Ruth and Bill Kaysing have compiled these recipes with one basic thought in mind: People don't like over-processed foods and they can save a lot of money by taking things into their own hands. These are practical recipes because they advise the cook where to find the necessary ingredients at low cost. And every bit as important — the food that you make will taste delicious! This is a companion volume to the book *Eat Well for 99¢ A Meal.* Even in these days when the price of seemingly everything is inflated beyond belief or despair, 99¢ can go a long way toward feeding a person who is willing to save money by providing the labor for processing food. *1996, 5½ x 8½, 272 pp, indexed, soft cover.* $14.95.

THE HYDROPONIC HOT HOUSE
Low-Cost, High-Yield Greenhouse Gardening
by James B. DeKorne

An illustrated guide to alternative-energy green-house gardening. Includes directions for building several different greenhouses, practical advice on harnessing solar energy, and many hard-earned suggestions for increasing plant yield. This is the first easy-to-use guide to home hydroponics. This hard-core working manual for the serious gardener is fully illustrated with diagrams, charts, and photographs. *1992, 5½ x 8½, 178 pp, illustrated, indexed, soft cover.* $16.95.

You can get these books at your favorite bookstore or contact any of our distributors:

Bookpeople
7900 Edgewater Drive
Oakland, CA 94261
1-800-999-4650

Homestead Books
6101 22nd Avenue NW
Seattle, WA 98107
1-800-426-6777

Ingram Book Company
One Ingram Blvd.
La Vergne, TN 37086-1986
1-800-937-8000

Last Gasp of San Francisco
777 Florida Street
San Francisco, CA 94110
1-415-824-6636

Left Bank Distribution
1004 Turner Way East
Seattle, WA 98112
1-206-322-2868

Loompanics Unlimited
PO Box 1197
Port Townsend, WA 98368
1-800-380-2230

Marlin's Book Distribution
19741 41st Avenue NE
Seattle, WA 98155
1-206-306-7187